Basic Tool Box

Teaching Basic Tools, Knowledge, and Skills for Anyone Ages 5 to 95

WRITTEN & ILLUSTRATED

BY

ROGER M. HAMMOND

Published by Create Space
North Charlestown, S.C.

ISBN - 13: 978 - 1540870797
ISBN - 10: 1540870790

DETAILS BY
Betsey Child
Lasting Impressions Graphic Studio
P. O. Box 1134
Enfield, NH 03748
603.632.9307
betsey-last-imp@comcast.net

TABLE OF CONTENTS

Mr Fix-It opened his first repair shop in 1978. The old three-story apartment house where they lived was built in the 1800's and had a stone slate roof. At that time, fix-it shops were unheard of in Keene, New Hampshire. With a wraparound drive, parking area for six cars, and a walk-in cellar basement, this was an ideal spot for a home business.

At the same time, over 3000 miles away in Los Angeles, California, a small company called "Harbor Freight Tools" was celebrating their first year anniversary. One of the company's main advertising piece was a black and white Tools for Sale flier mailed out all across the U. S.

After reading the flier, Mr Fix-it called in a hand tool order. When the hand tools promptly arrived, the excellent quality of each tool was impressive. Wow! There has been a lot of water over the dam since 1978 for Mr Fix-It and for Harbor Freight Tools.

Harbor Freight Tools has over 30 million customers who shop 300+ store nationwide and order on line.

Mr. Fix-It has bought, sold and used Harbor Freight tools for over 40 years. Each one of their stores and catalogs are a must-see or visit for everyone 5 to 95.

An Open Letter From the Author

The importance of basic tool knowledge and skill has no real age boundaries. From the very young to the very old, there is a need to know and understand basic tools. While teaching my own children which tools were needed for just the right job, an awareness of the need to have a book of basic tools became apparent.

I hope this book can fill your home with joy, good basic knowledge on the use of hand tools, and happy smiles from everyone who uses this Basic Tool Box Book.

My first and foremost goal in writing this book was to provide a reference guide that all of you can use to better yourselves as tool handlers, and a guide that would give you more confidence in your abilities.

Patience, care, and kindness, should accompany you and your children when reading and practicing the skills in this Basic Tool Box Book.

My daughter Beth, who inspired me to write this book.

Peter, my son at age 5, helping me in the workshop.

The First Edition of this book was self-published in 1983

iii

DEDICATION

I am dedicating this book, **"Basic Tool Box",** to my son Peter and daughter Beth.

When I was a small boy of five, I learned many wonderful ways to use tools from my grandfather. Our Grandpa, your great-grandpa, was a good carpenter and a hard worker, as you can see in the pictures below. He built his own home on a country road in Vermont.

In the picture above, Grandpa and his children are digging – by hand – the foundation for their new house. At the right are the finished house and garage.

Love, Dad

KNOW YOUR BASIC TOOLS

Before anyone can take anything apart, or fix any item, you should know what the tools are. I suggest you hold them and touch them. Look at every part of each tool and learn how it moves and works.

This Section regarding Basic Tools will help you learn about many different kinds of tools. There will be pictures of each tool we talk about.

If you have your own tools, you will be able to better understand what we are talking about. Many grownups have hand tools, and also many of your friends may have tools, that they will share with you if you do not have your own.

You may want to put hand tools on your list for Santa

. . . or for your birthday.

On weekends when I was very young, I would stand holding Grandpa's coverall pants leg and watch wide-eyed while he worked. It was a lot of fun watching the wood chips fall all around me as Grandpa made things like bird houses and old-fashioned rubber-band guns.

Of course Grandpa could repair almost anything!

He also saved every nut and bolt and piece of wire. The two-bay garage he built was filled with jars that had lids nailed to rotating boards. In each jar were many hardward treasures.

My favorite times as a child were spent with Grandpa who would teach me how to use hand tools. These lessons were skills that had been taught to him by his father, were passed on to me, and now on to you!

On special days, like Christmas and birthdays, I received hand tools: first screwdrivers, then pliers, and finally, a special box – a home for my first tools.

(Beth, today I am rewriting my first book called "Beth Ann's Tool Box" written in memory of this special day – 32 years later. In 1984 you were the same age that I was when I first stood holding my Grandpa's pant leg. ~ Love, Dad)

In memory of this special day, I have written this simple book on the basic tools and skills you will need as you, and all children, grow older.

When you are by yourself, you can look at all the pictures, but you will need help from an adult when handling each tool and learning all I have written. We will add a DVD in the next book: "Basic and Power Tools".

Good luck,
Mr. Fix-it

THE TOOL BOX FAMILY
A home for your tools

#1: The Tool Box

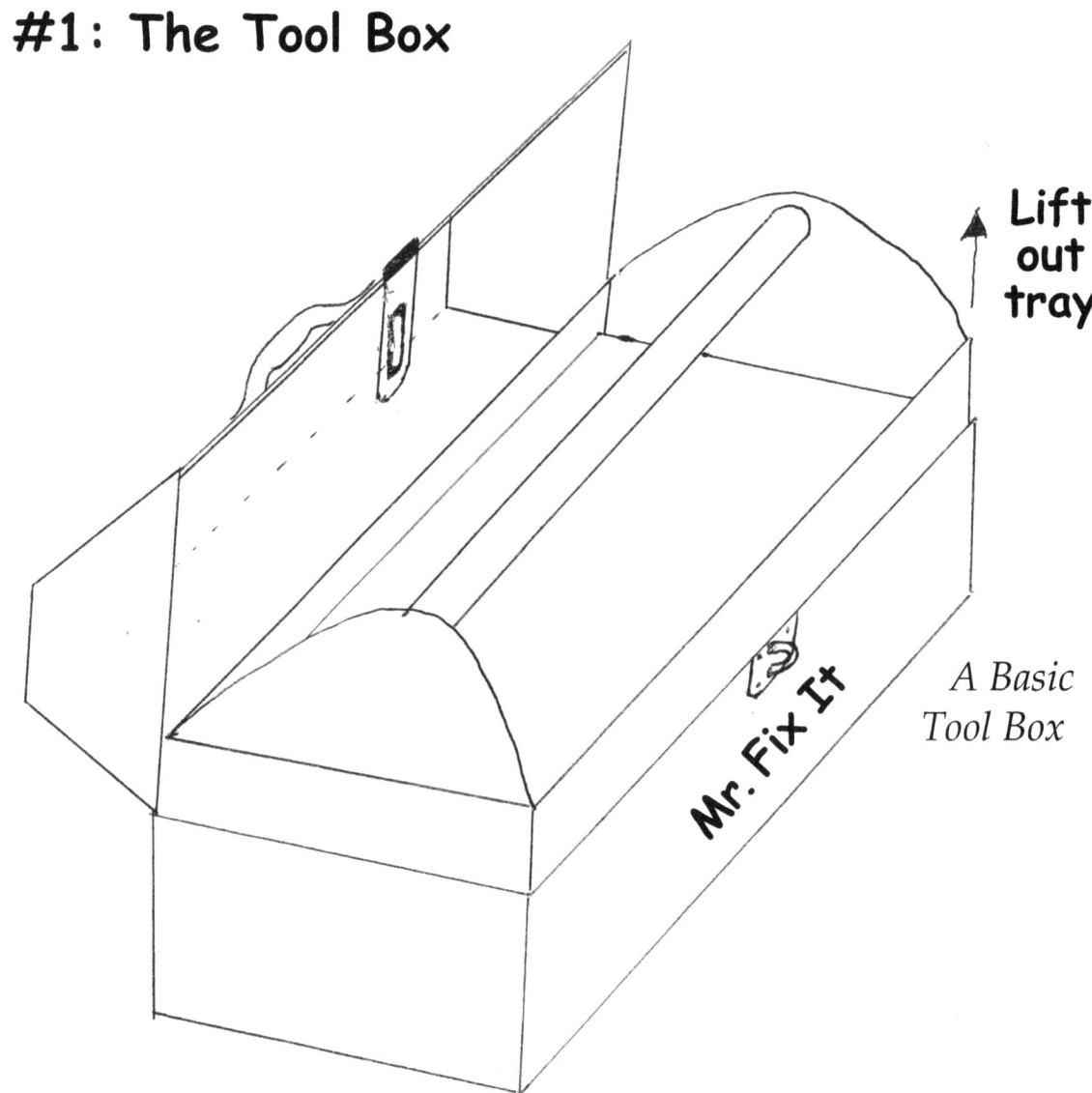

Lift out tray

A Basic Tool Box

Mr. Fix It

THE BASIC TOOL BOX is the home for all your new tools. It should have a tray that can be taken out, and a locking lid with a handle. This type of toolbox will keep your tools from getting lost. Paint or print your name on the side (mine is "Mr. Fix It") and keep it in a dry place.

RULE OF THUMB: The toolbox must be large enough for your hammer and hack saw which we will talk about shortly.

THE SCREWDRIVER FAMILY

#2, #3, #4:
Common Screwdrivers

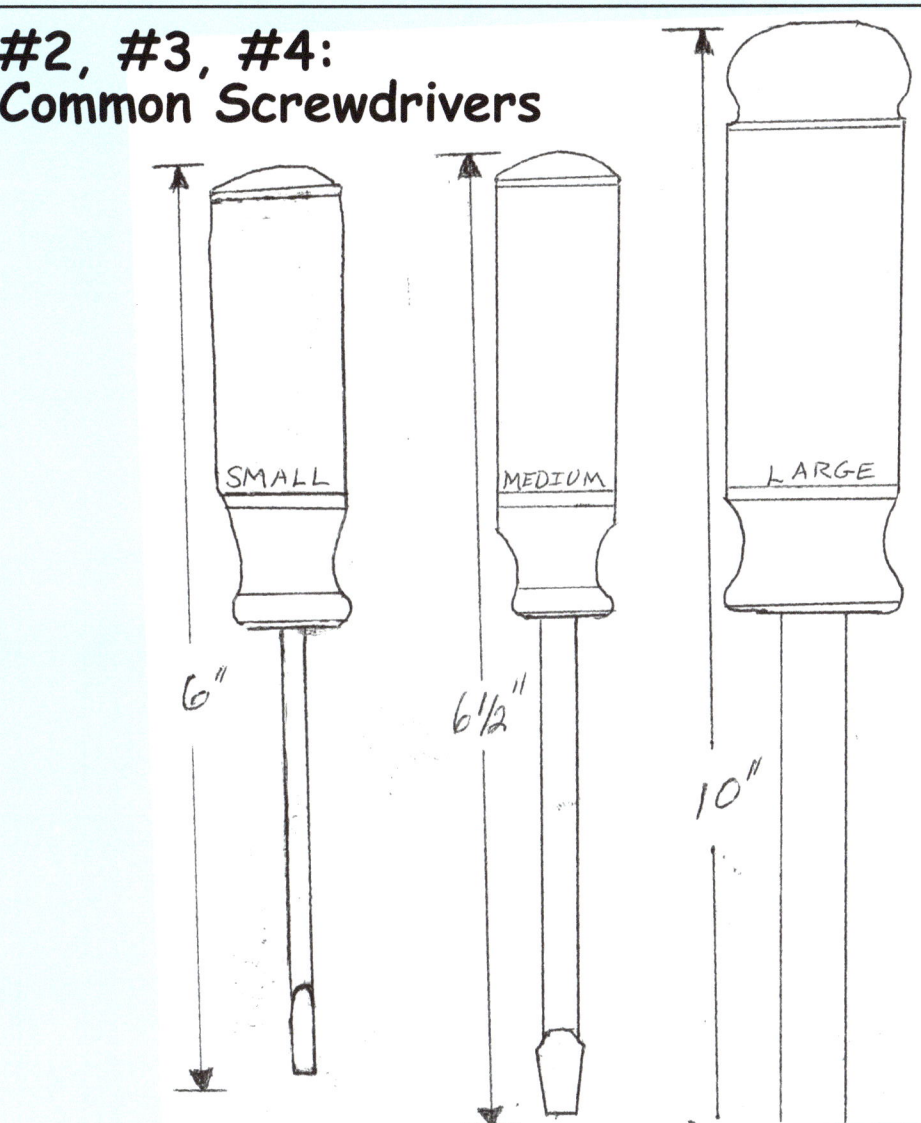

COMMON SCREWDRIVERS come in many sizes and shapes. Common screwdrivers have flat ends and fit into common screws. (They have one line/slot on the head, or top, of the screw.)

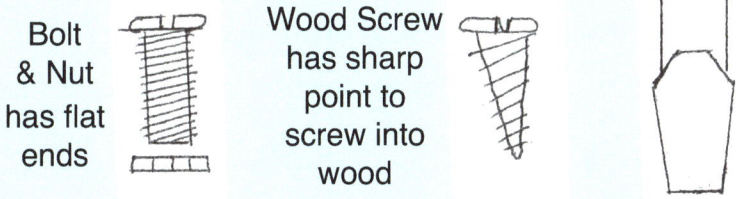 *RULE OF THUMB: You need three sizes of Common Screwdrivers for your basic tool box: small, medium, and large.*

Bolt & Nut has flat ends

Wood Screw has sharp point to screw into wood

#5, #6: Phillips Screwdrivers

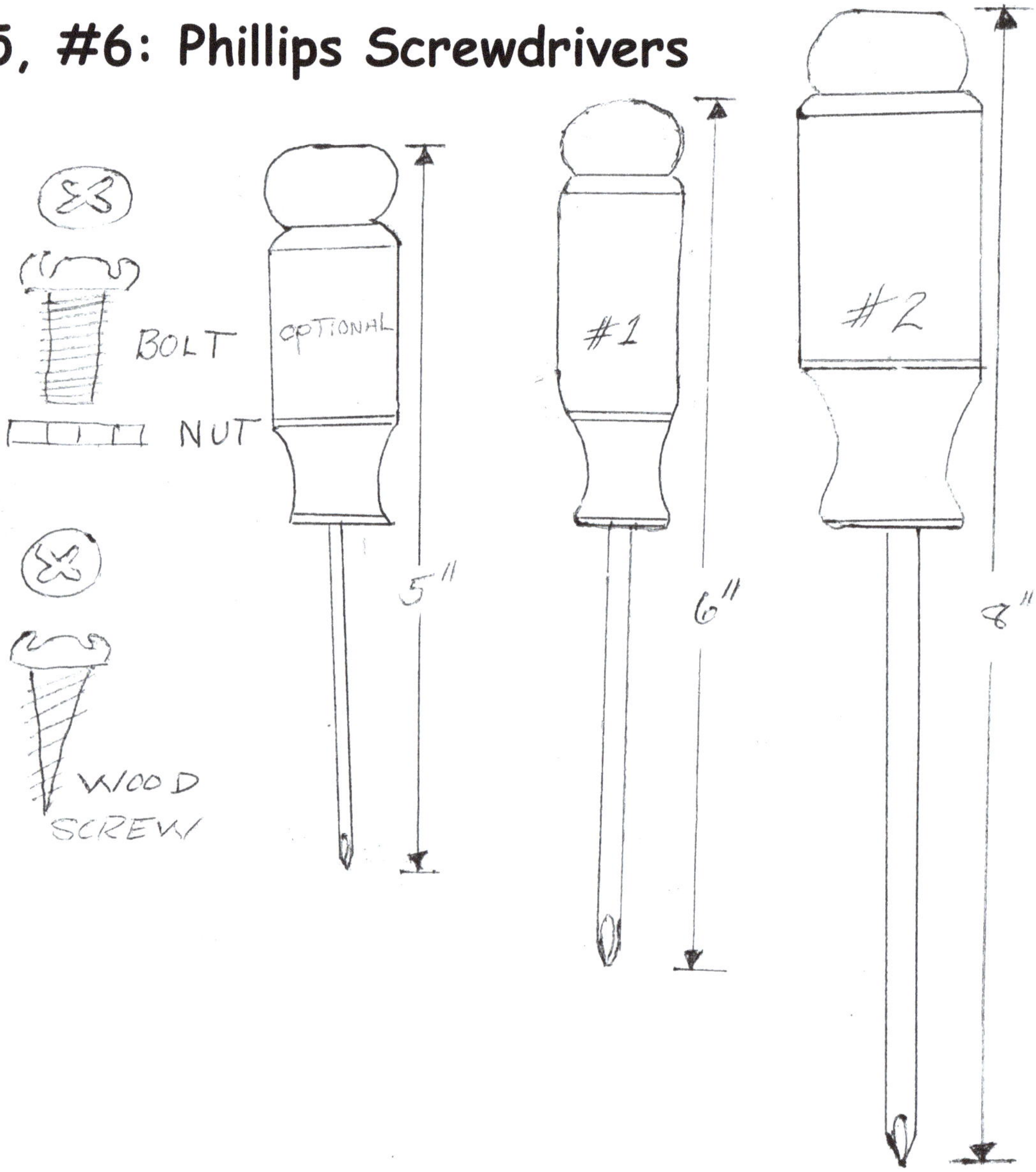

BOLT

NUT

WOOD SCREW

OPTIONAL

5"

#1

6"

#2

8"

PHILLIPS SCREWDRIVERS are also varied in size and shape. We can tell Phillips Screwdrivers are different from Common Screwdrivers by looking at the "**X**" shaped end and heads of screws with **X** on them.

There are many Phillips screws around your house that you must use your Phillips screwdriver to take out or put in.

Later in the book you will play detective and find some.

 RULE OF THUMB: You'll need all three sizes in your basic tool box.

#7: Multi-Tip Screwdrivers

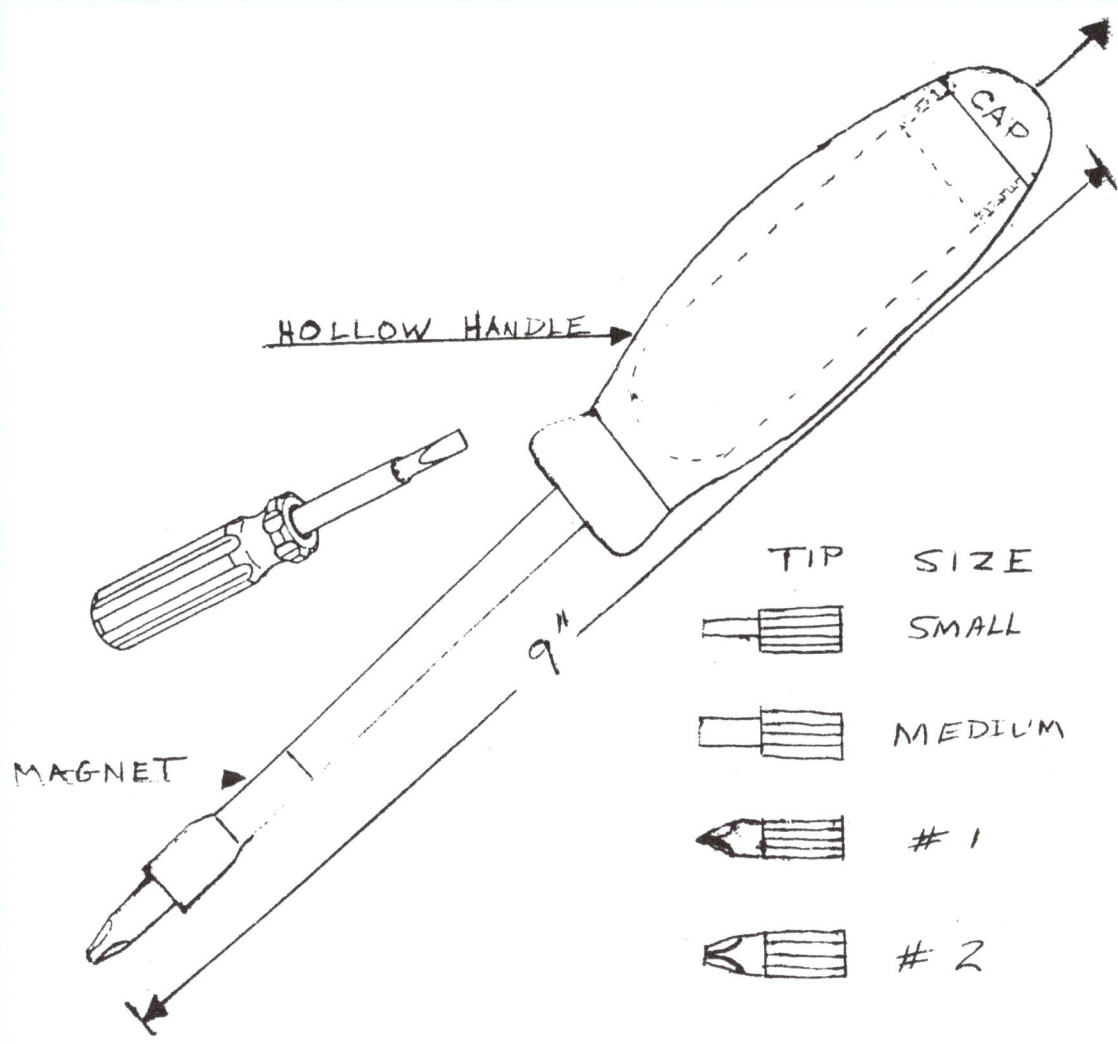

MULTI-TIP SCREWDRIVERS are a handy tool for your basic tool box. Some have secret magnets hidden deep in the screwdriver that hold the individual tips to the end. More tips are stored in the handle. To change tips, pull one out and push in another.

RULE OF THUMB: This is an excellent tool to practice with and to learn the different screwdriver types. A multi-tip screwdriver is easy to work with. (If it is magnetic and has a handle storage compartment, that's great.).

#8: Jeweler's Screwdriver Set

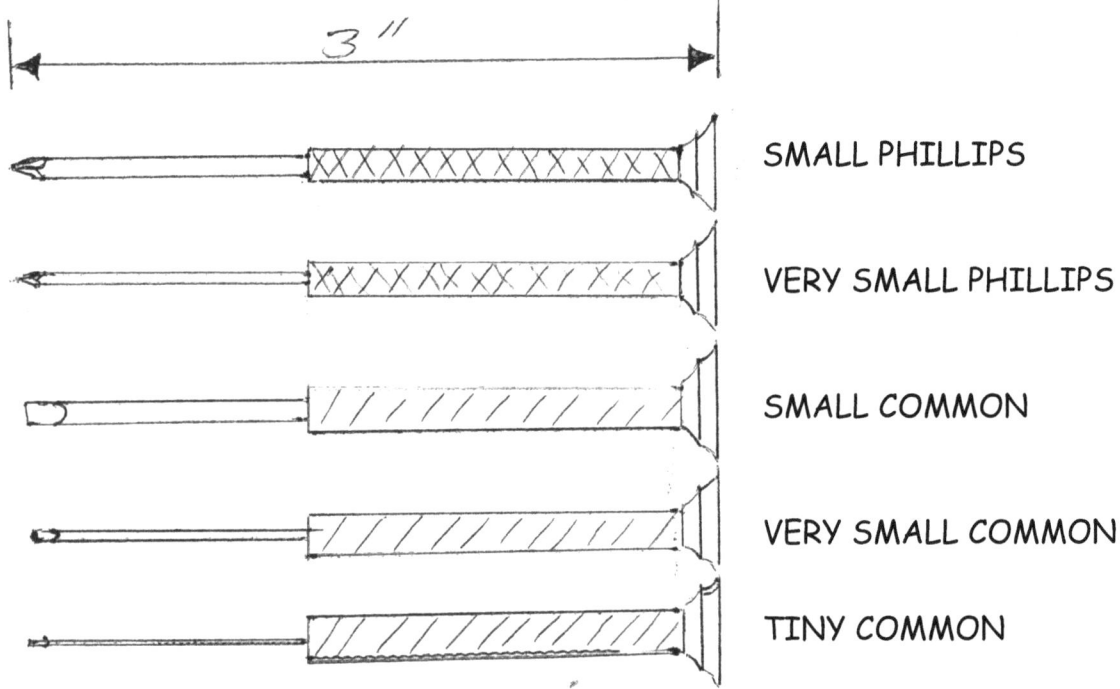

3″

SMALL PHILLIPS

VERY SMALL PHILLIPS

SMALL COMMON

VERY SMALL COMMON

TINY COMMON

JEWELERS' SCREWDRIVERS are very tiny and are used to work on small toys, eyeglasses, watches and even small radios, etc. They come in sets. There are usually five screwdrivers in each set, and include three common screwdrivers and two tiny Phillips screwdrivers.

RULE OF THUMB: Always keep these tiny screwdrivers in a case or small plastic box. Most new sets come in their own special case. Because they are so tiny, they are very easy to lose.

THE HAMMER FAMILY

#9: Hammer

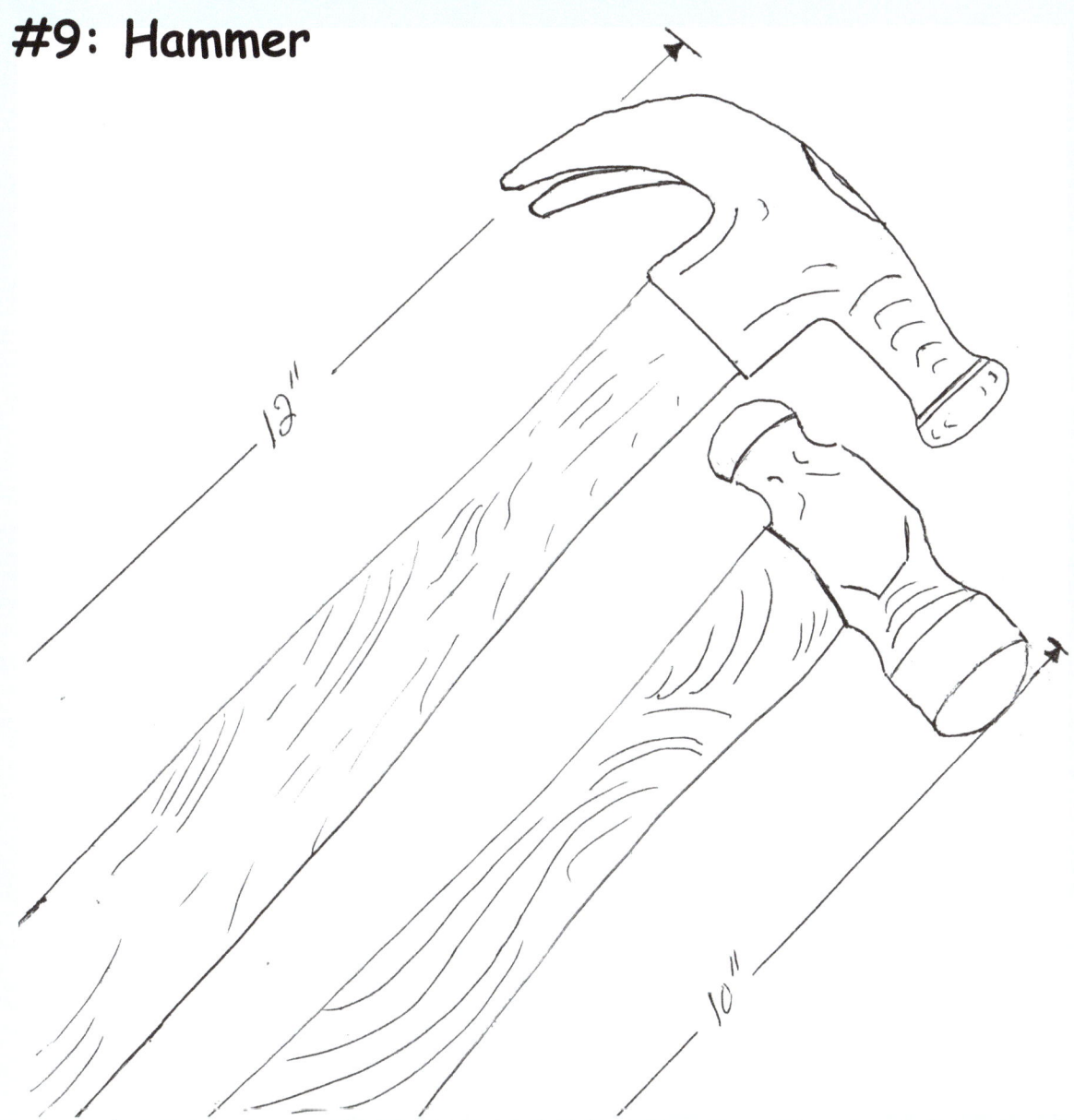

HAMMERS are an important part of your basic toolbox. A large carpenter's claw hammer will not fit into a small tool box, so a lightweight claw hammer (12″ above) is recommended, or you can substitute a ball pein hammer (10″ above).

RULE OF THUMB: Wooden hammer handles are easy to grab and hold, and are light in weight. They are often less expensive.

THE SAW FAMILY

#10: Hacksaw

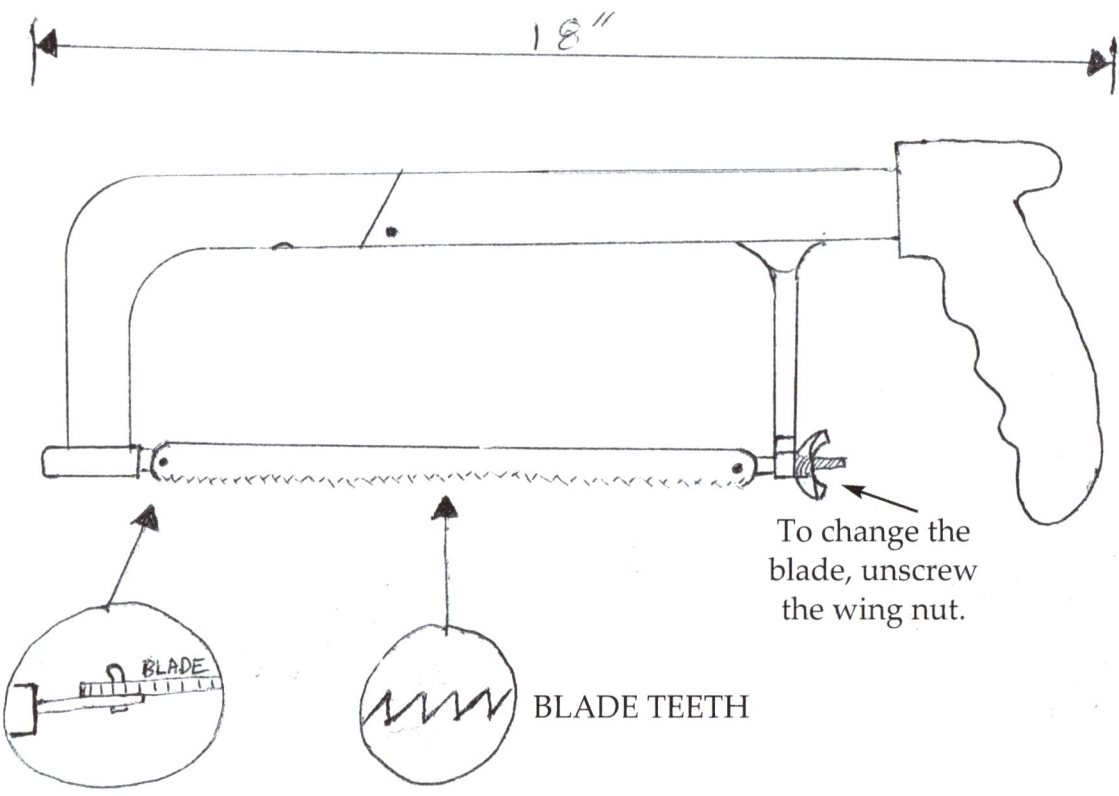

18"

To change the
blade, unscrew
the wing nut.

BLADE

BLADE TEETH

HACKSAWS are designed to cut metal objects like pipe, heavy wire and large nails. Hacksaws will also easily cut wood and plastic pipes. Hacksaws should only be used when an adult is present, as they are very sharp. The blade teeth must be on the bottom and face forward.

RULE OF THUMB: *Always have two blades. Blades break easily. You should ask for help from an adult when using your hacksaw.*

THE PLIER FAMILY

#11: Common Pliers

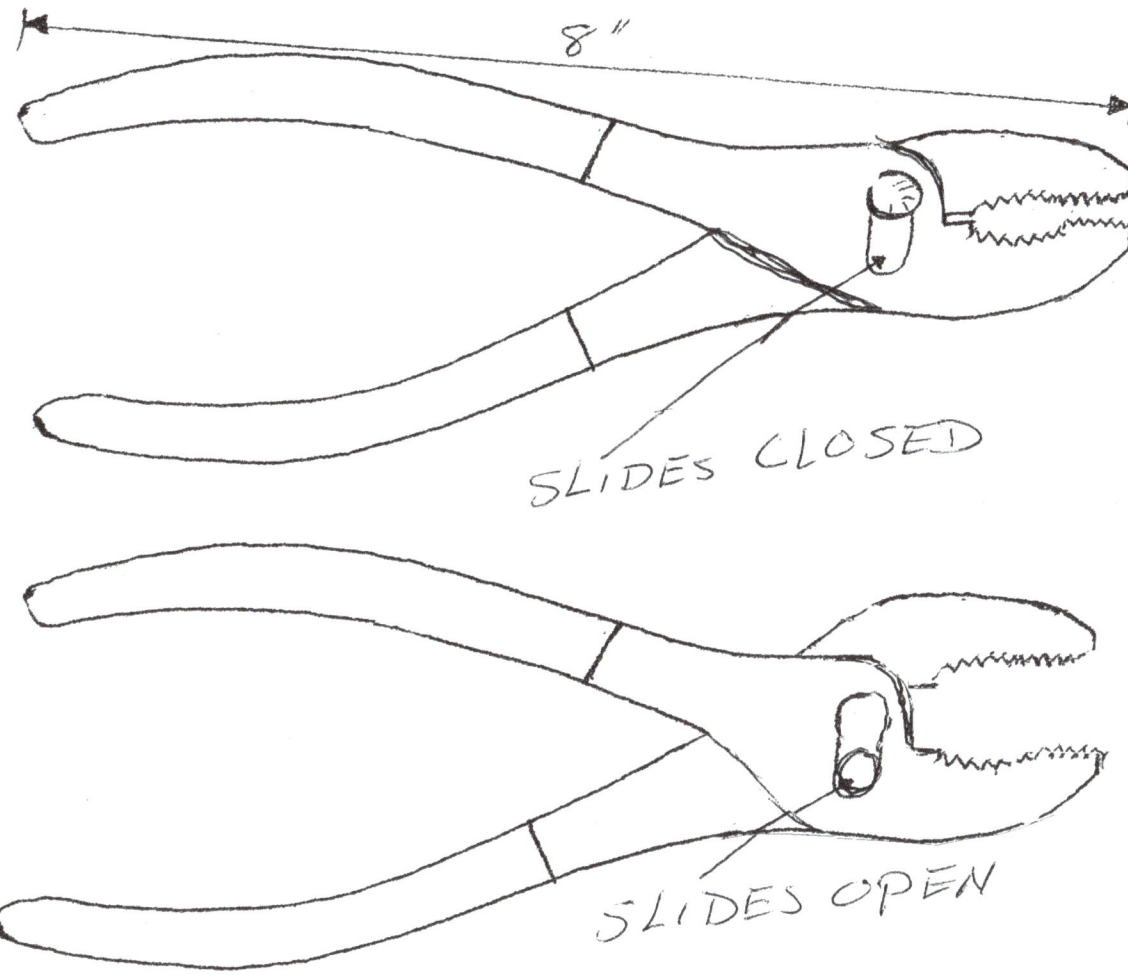

8"

SLIDES CLOSED

SLIDES OPEN

COMMON PLIERS are the most all-around-used tool. They are used to pinch, grip, hold, bite, and squash (crimp) many thngs.

RULE OF THUMB: Common Pliers should have gripping type teeth in the entire mouth (see above). They should be a size you can handle easily, and they should have a two-position slide, which means they will open to a larger size when needed.

#12: Vise-Grip Pliers

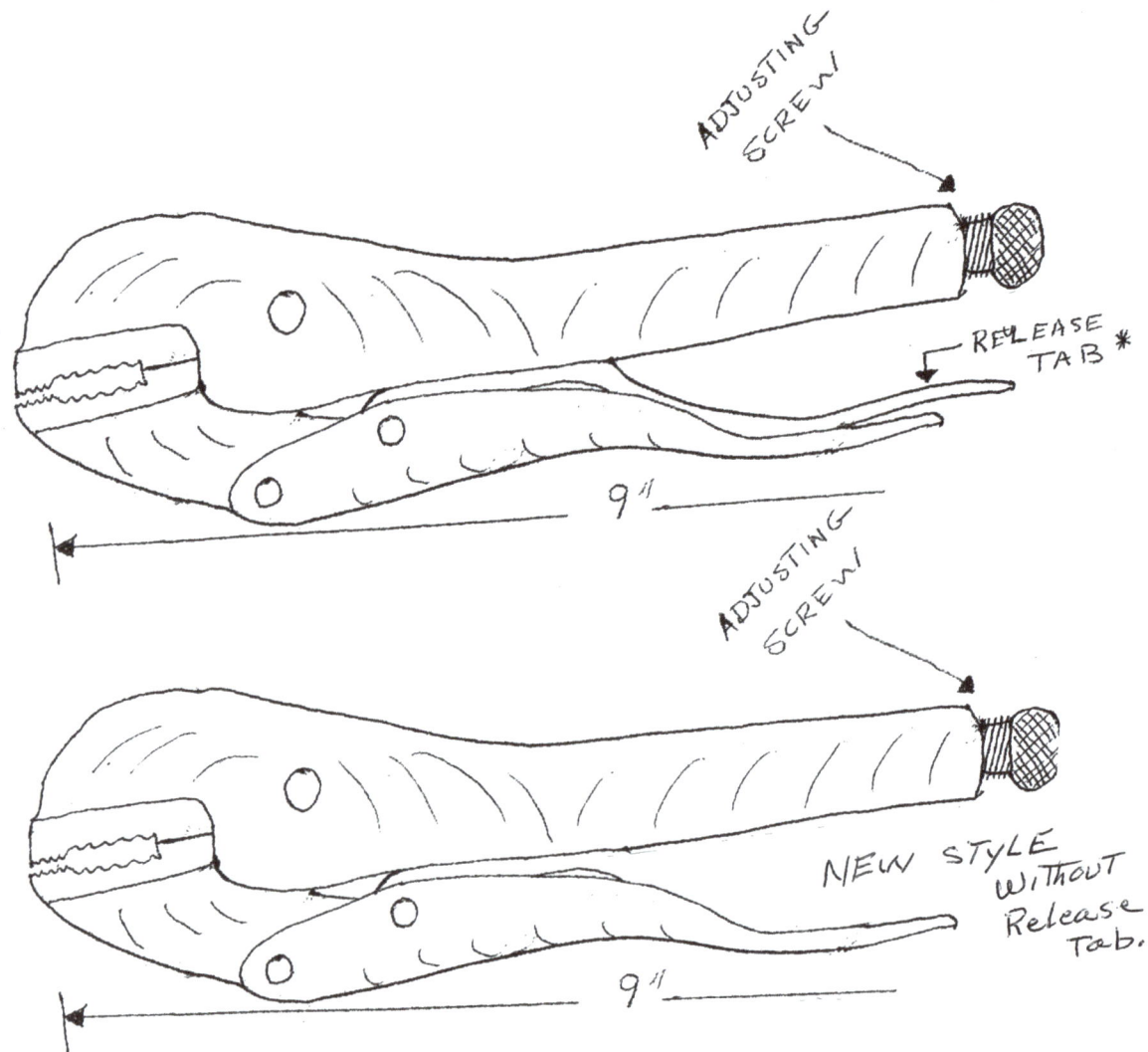

VISE-GRIP PLIERS are very handy tools. By adjusting a large screw in the back of the vise-grip, you can set the jaw opening to any size. Then when the pliers are closed and shut, they won't come open. This is great for locking two things together and holding them.

RULE OF THUMB: The jaw area should have teeth and there should be a release tab* to unlock the pliers. There are also more Vise-Grip Pliers without release tabs that work just fine.

#13: Long Nose Pliers

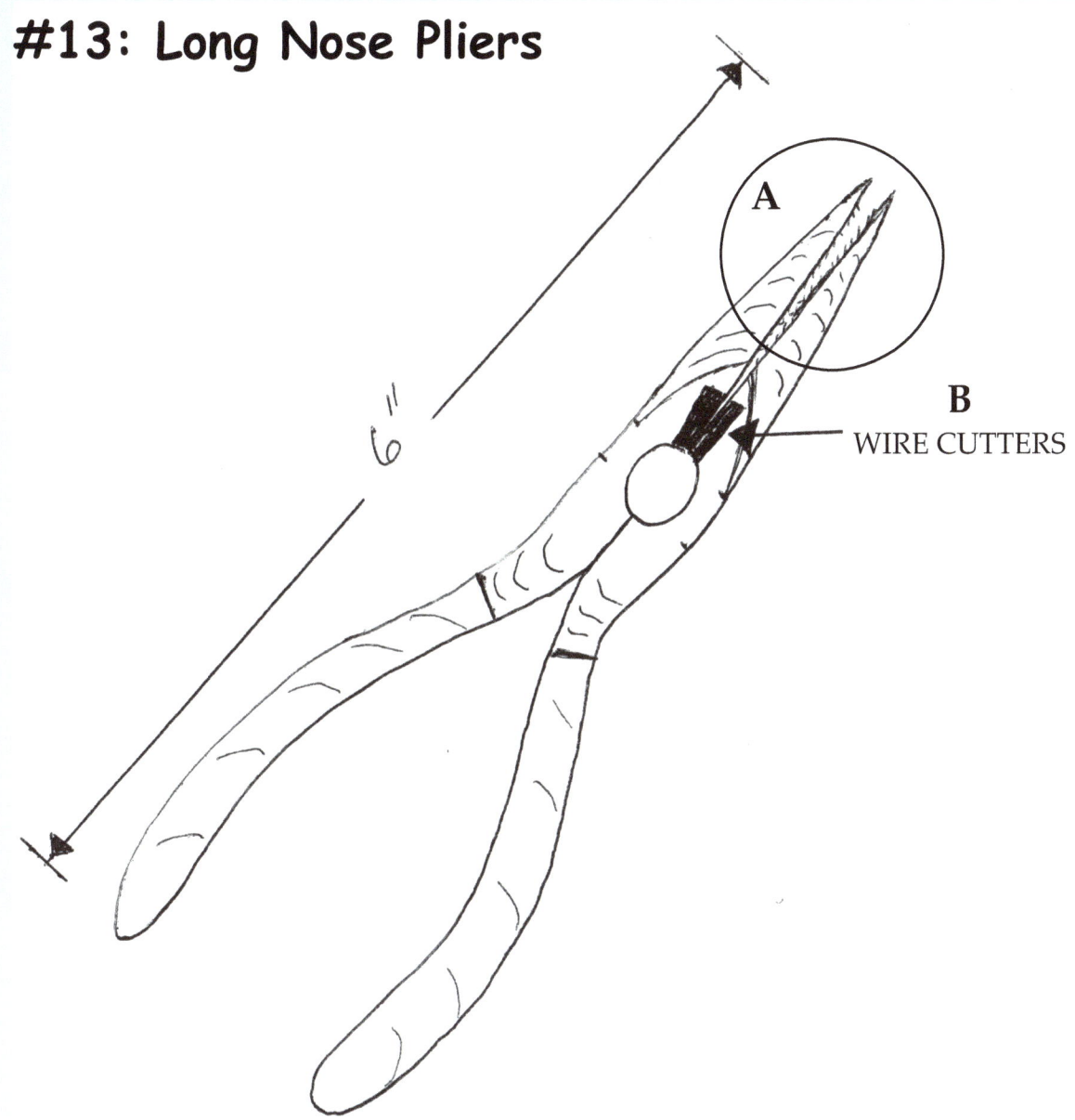

LONG NOSE PLIERS are an excellent hobby tool. They can be used for everything from holding small parts on all types of models and crafts, for woodworking, or for flower arranging. The long nose pliers are a must when working with small wire and tiny parts.

RULE OF THUMB: The mouth should have teeth (A) the entire length , and also have a wire-cutter section (B).

#14: Tweezers

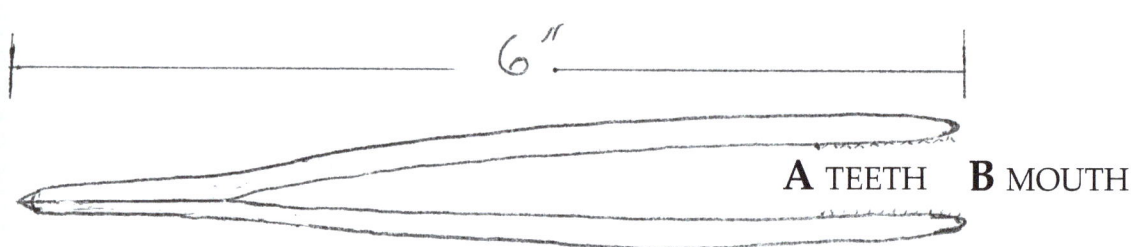

A TEETH   B MOUTH

TWEEZERS can be the common household type – like those found in your family medicine cabinet, or in a first aid kit. Tweezers are used to get small things out of small holes, and to handle small parts.

RULE OF THUMB: Tweezers should be at least 4-6 inches long and have small teeth (A) in the front section of the mouth (B).

#15: Wire Cutters

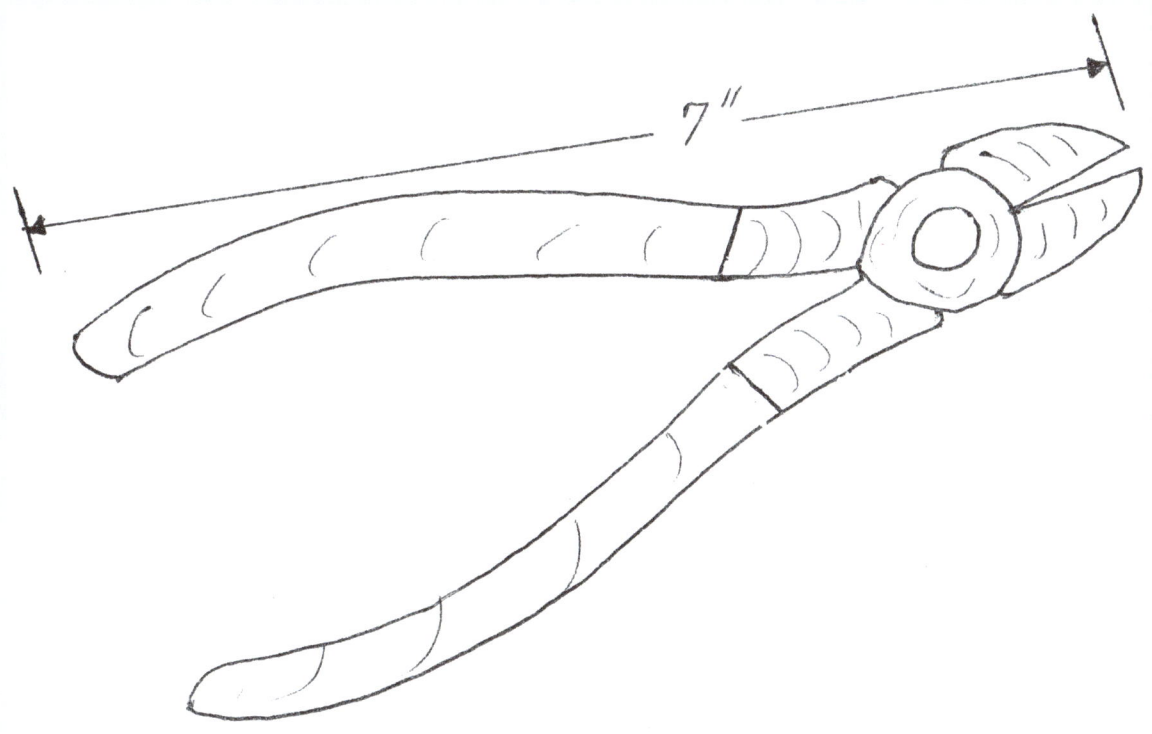

7"

WIRE CUTTERS are a must when cutting cord, wire, and small pipe. Wire cutters are the only pliers that will cut wire that is laying on a flat surface, or that is inside a hole or a box. Usually, wire cutters will not cut large items or hardened steel objects. These large items can be held securely with the use of vise-grips and cut off using a hacksaw.

RULE OF THUMB: People often have wire cutters that are too small. If you own a pair of wire cutters that seem a little too large for you, they are probably the size you need.

#16: Sta-Kon Pliers

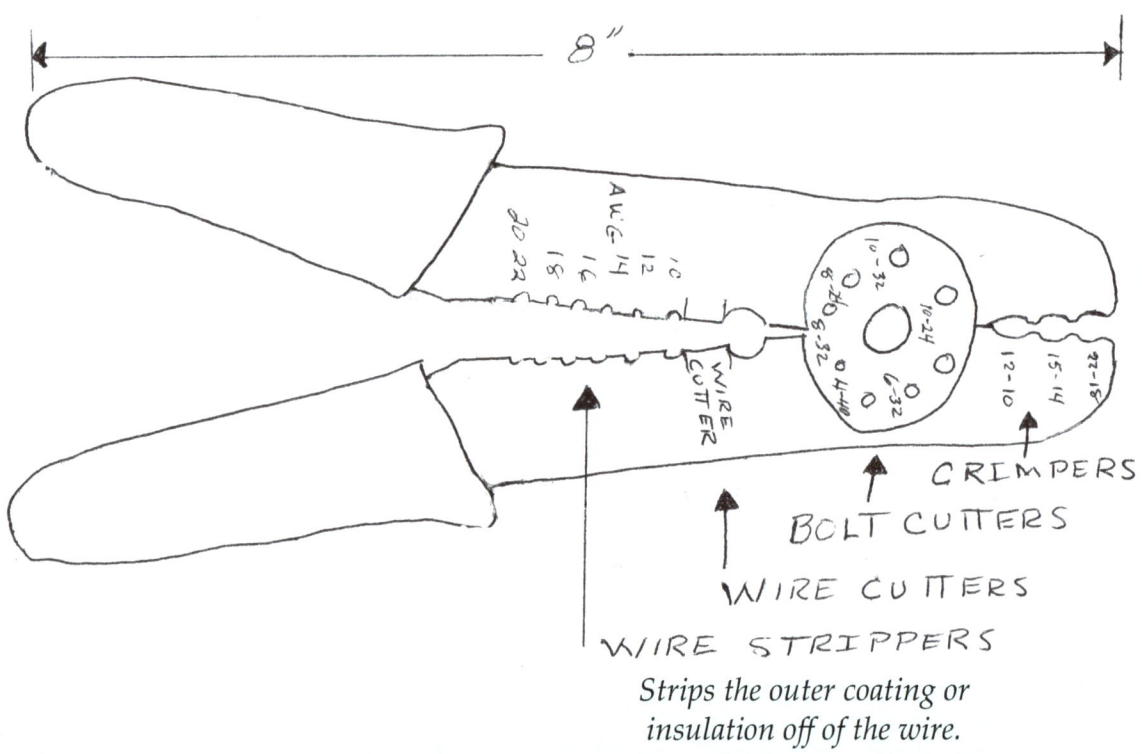

WIRE STRIPPERS

Strips the outer coating or insulation off of the wire.

STA-KON PLIERS are four tools in one. The four things that they do are: cut wire, strip insulation off wires, cut bolts, and crimp (squash) Sta-Kon connectors. These pliers are a very important tool for your basic toolbox. As you practice with them, you will rely on them more and more.

RULE OF THUMB: Brand name pliers are usually better (those made by companies specializing in making tools). They have been made using a higher quality, stronger steel, and will last longer.

THE SCRIBE FAMILY

#17: Steel Scribe

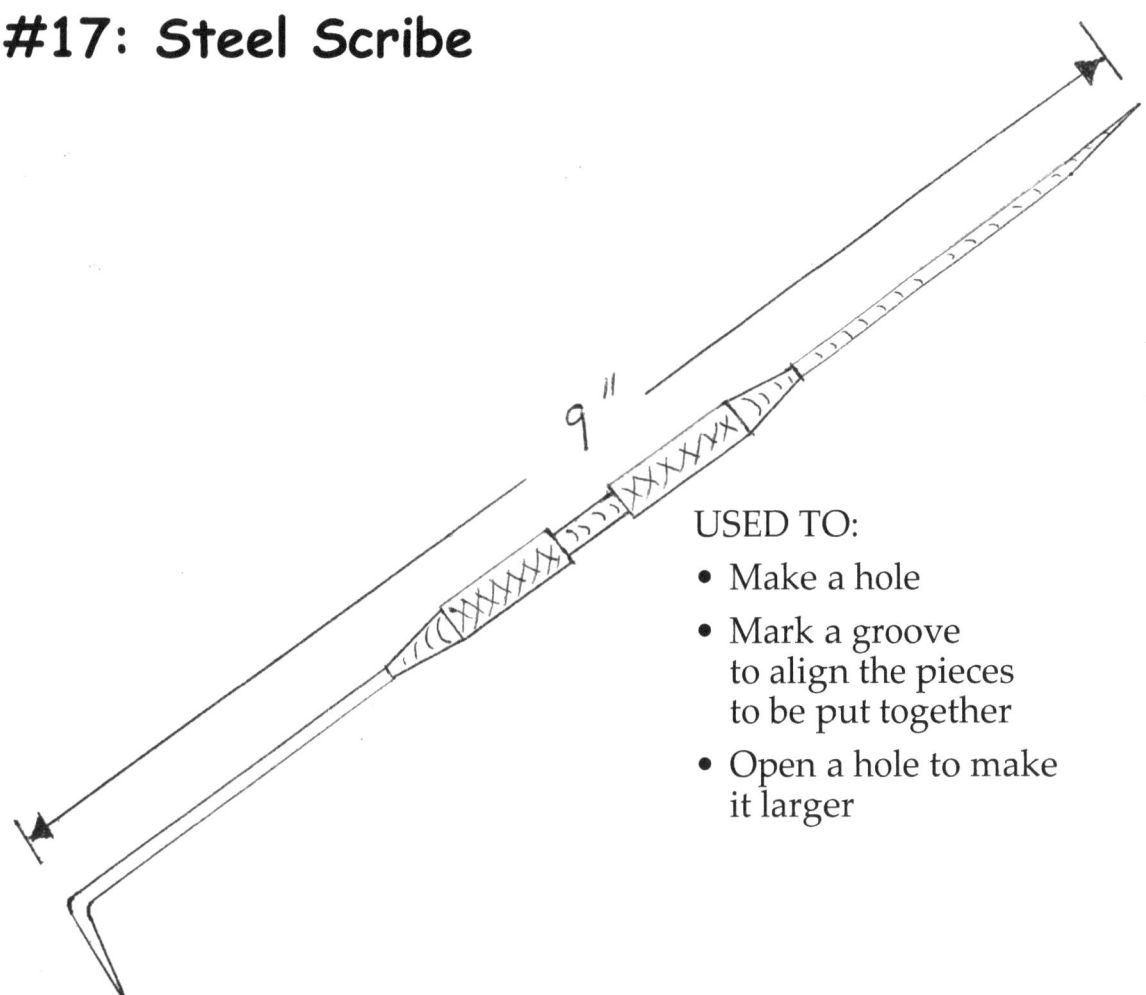

9"

USED TO:
- Make a hole
- Mark a groove
  to align the pieces
  to be put together
- Open a hole to make
  it larger

STEEL SCRIBES are useful in cleaning parts, poking holes, and digging at many things. Scribes were originally designed for people who assembled part of machines. For example: let's say a motor was being put together, but before it could be assembled, it needed to be painted. A person could use the scribe to mark the places where the machine would be put together, and after the motor was painted, the assembler could find the marks and use them in joining the parts correctly together.

RULE OF THUMB: Your scribe should be of hardened steel and have a 90-degree hook at one end (see above).

THE FILE FAMILY

#18: IGNITION FILE

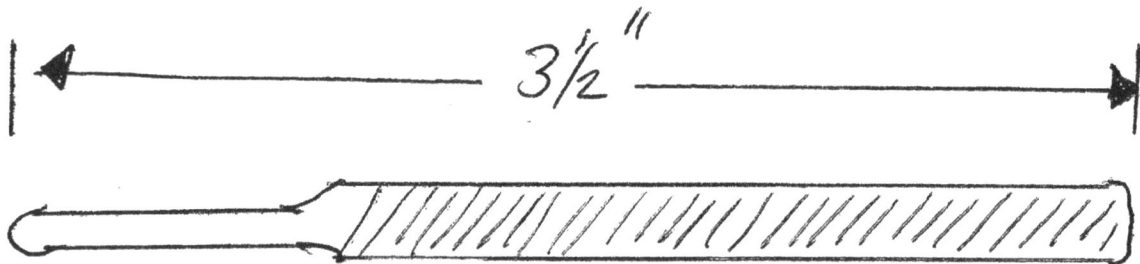

3½"

IGNITION FILES are very small and are used to rub off sharp objects, or to clean small parts.

RULE OF THUMB: *Most ignition files are inexpensive and are found at an auto parts store. Some are made of hard material like a fingernail file.*

#19: FLAT FILE

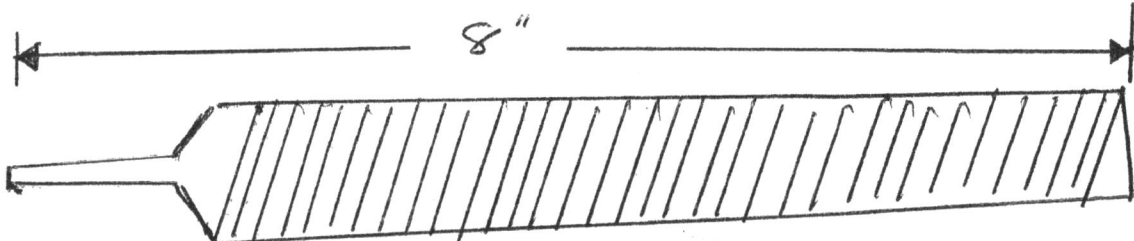

8"

FLAT FILES should be medium-to-rough, and about 8 inches in length. You will use this common household file to remove sharp corners and round off wooden items.

RULE OF THUMB: *Cleaning the file after each use is one of the Basic Tool Box Rules of Thumb. Clean and wipe off all tools before putting them back into your basic tool box. Also, replace any broken tool, or at least tell someone else that the tool is broken.*

THE WRENCH FAMILY

#20: Adjustable Wrench

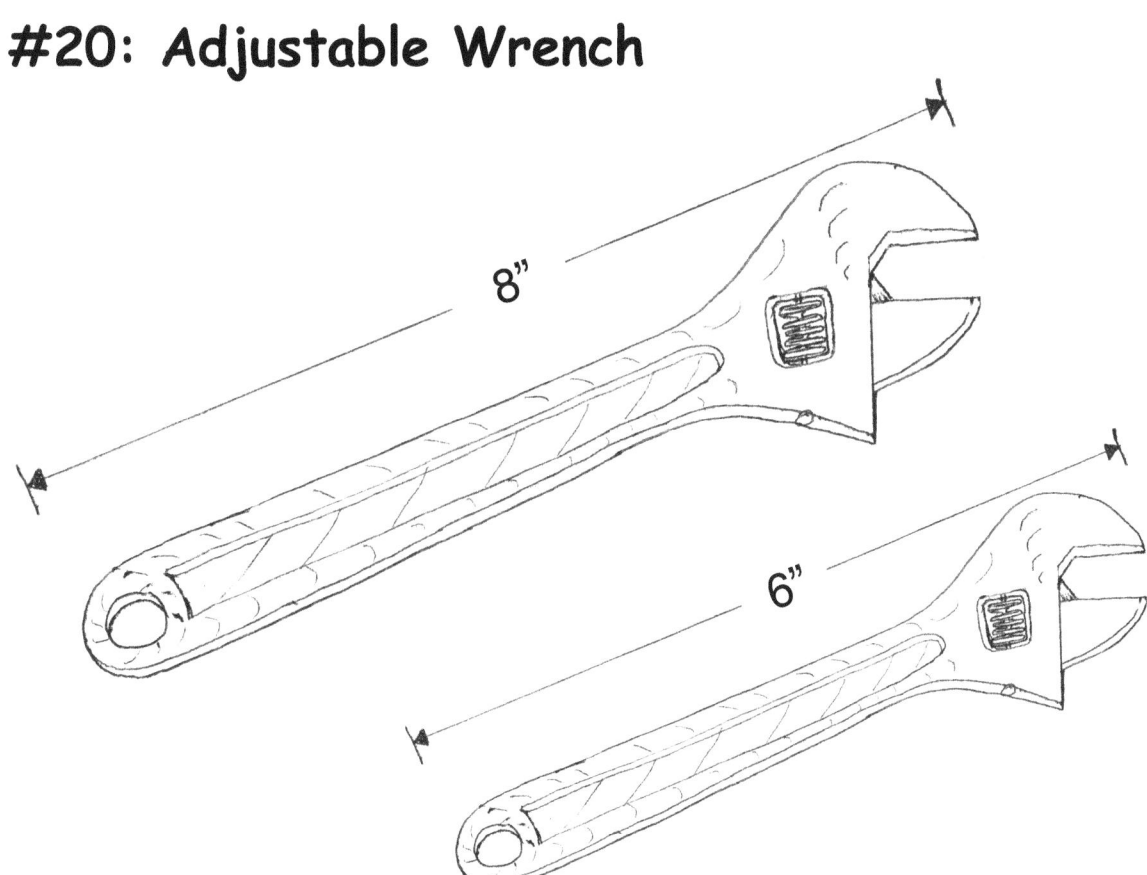

Both 6-inch and 8-inch ADJUSTABLE WRENCHES are needed to work on your bike, water pipes, lawn and yard tools, and on furniture such as swing sets. Wrenches are tools everyone uses and it will be hard for you not to fill your toolbox with all shapes and sizes of them. Remember that the adjustable wrench will fit standard and metric size hardware.

RULE OF THUMB: When buying an adjustable wrench, you should purchase a brand name, because you will be using this tool for many jobs, and you will want a well-made tool that will last a long time and open and close well. Less expensive adjustable wrenches bind up and are difficult to work with.

#21: Nut Driver Wrench Set

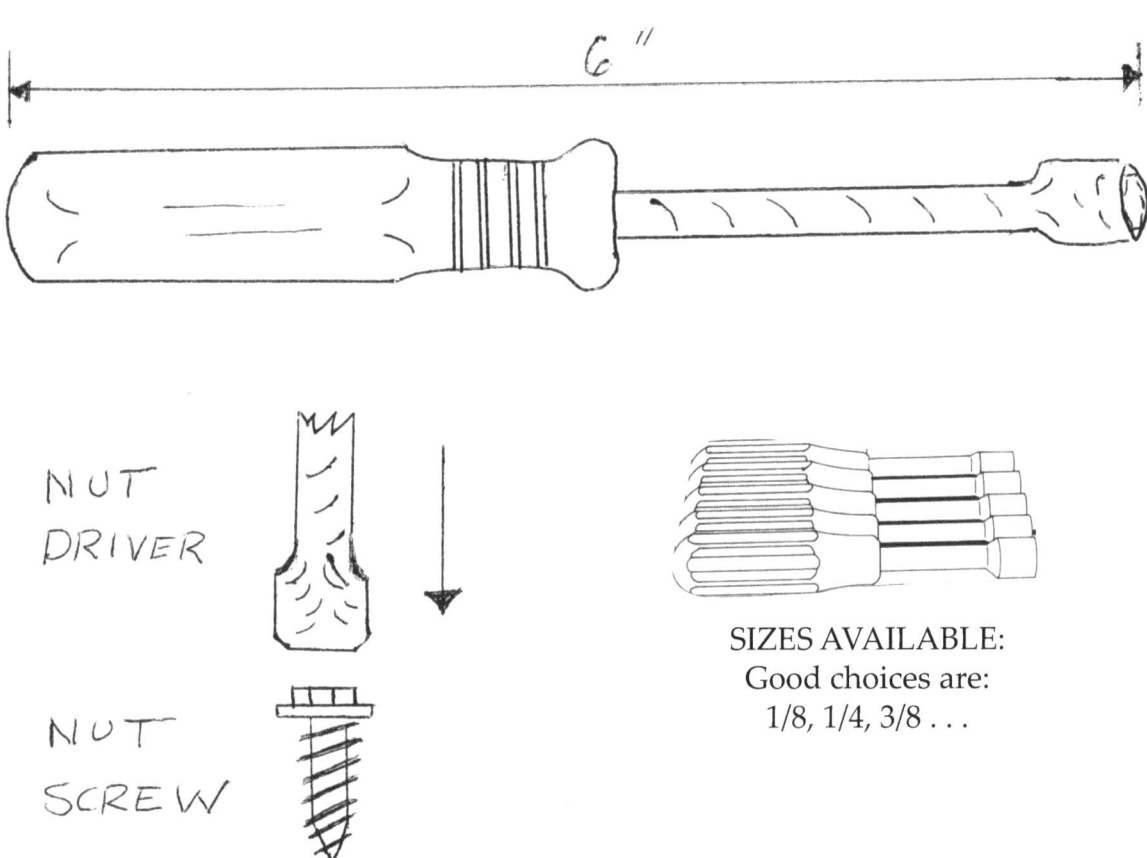

NUT DRIVER

NUT SCREW

SIZES AVAILABLE:
Good choices are:
1/8, 1/4, 3/8 . . .

   NUT DRIVER WRENCHES usually come in a set of five different sizes. They are used to screw nut-type screws in and out, or a nut on and off. Nut screws are found on most small appliances. See above for a picture of a nut driver wrench and nut driver screws.

   RULE OF THUMB: Stay away from kits where the wrenches are able to be pulled in and out of their handles ... buy wrenches where the wrench is solid and has a molded handle. Solid sets are the best and many times you can find good ones that do not cost much money.

THE PUNCH FAMILY

#22: Center Punches

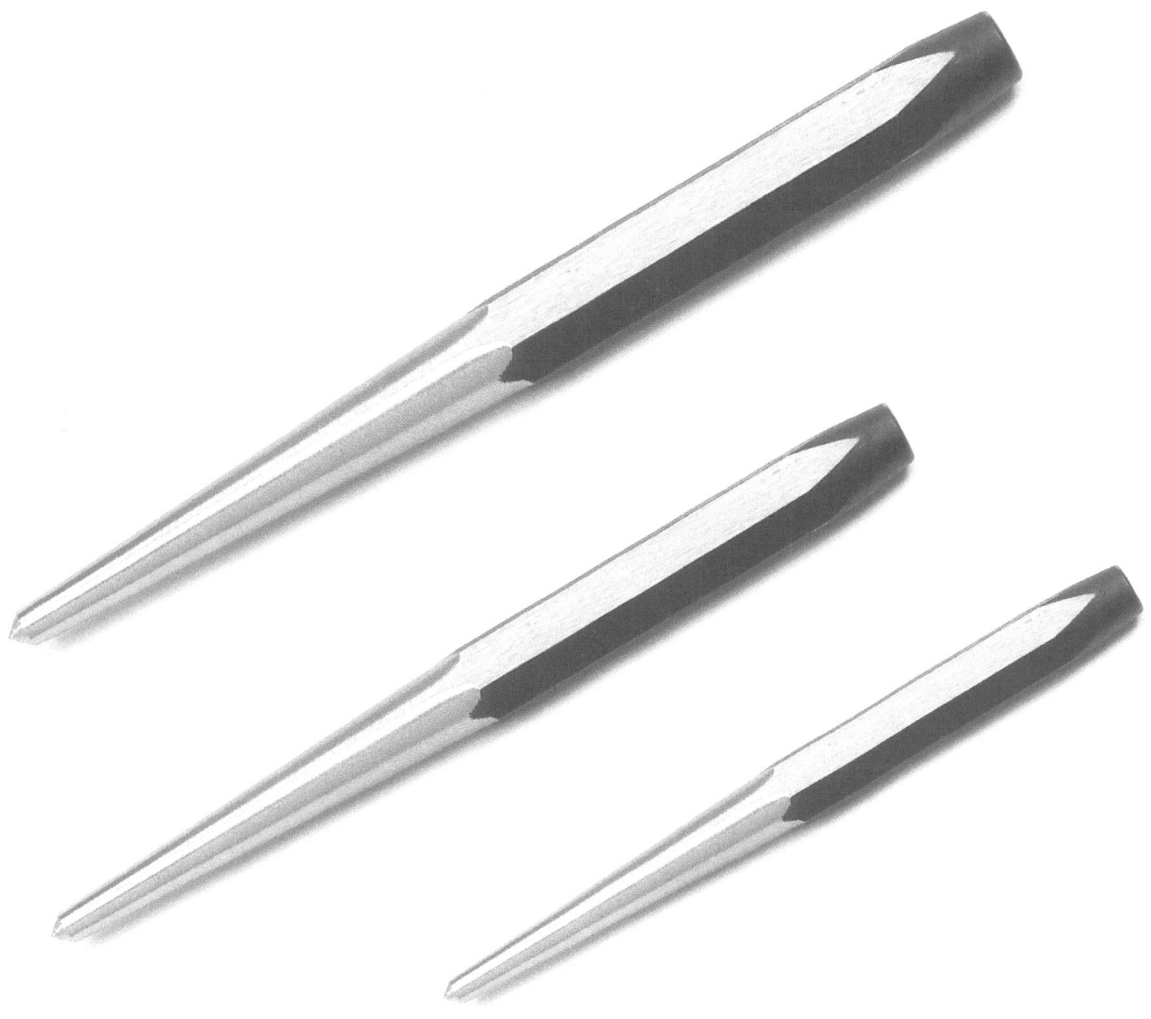

CENTER PUNCH all the spots where you are going to start a nail or screw. You can do this by holding the Center Punch with one hand pointing down, and hitting the opposite end of the punch with your hammer. Aren't you glad you have a light-weight hammer? Center punching is also used before starting to drill a hole.

RULE OF THUMB: This is another inexpensive tool, but it should be made of steel!

THE SCALE FAMILY

#23: Retractable Scale (Ruler)

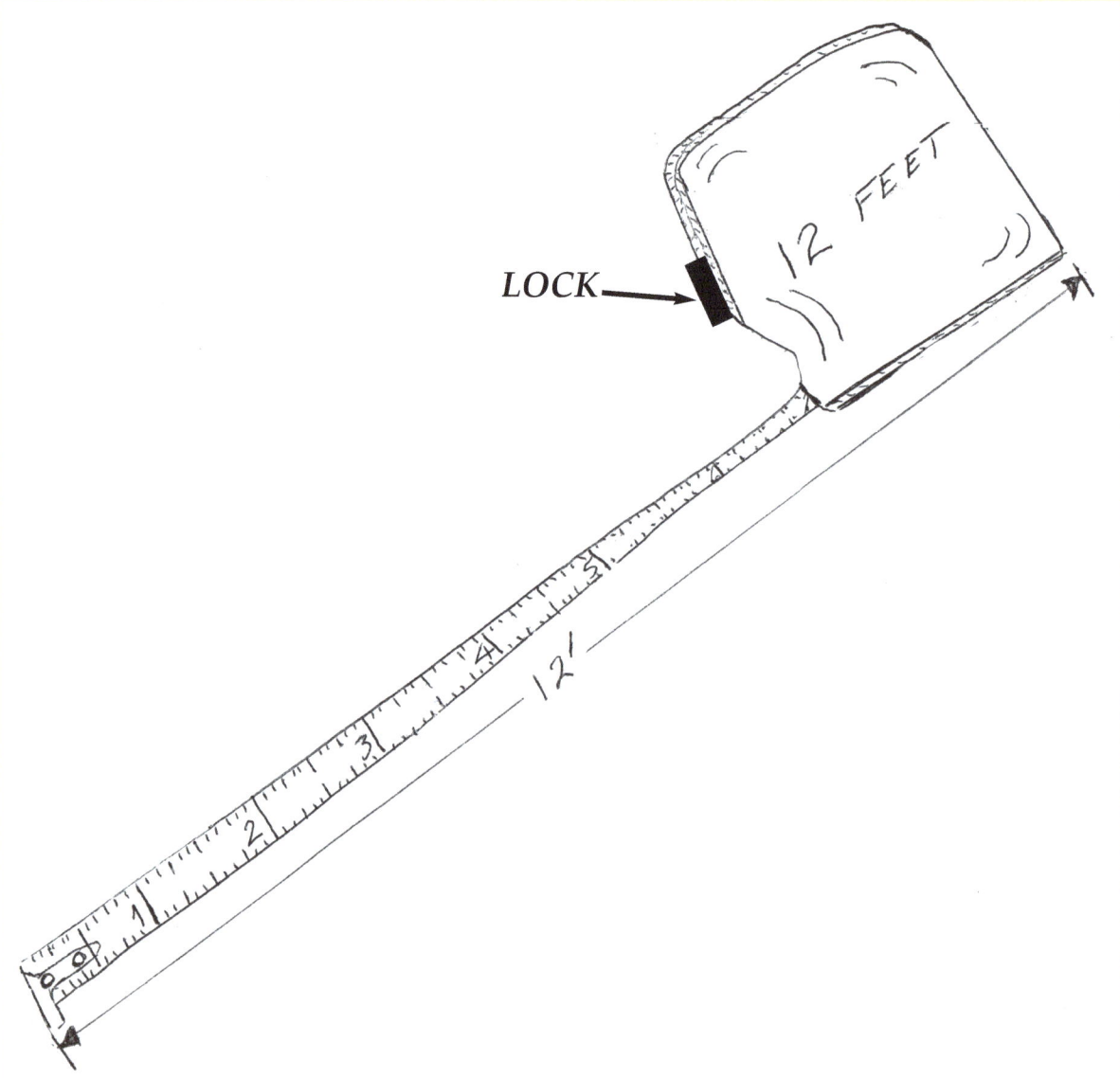

RETRACTABLE SCALES are handy when it comes to measuring most anything. Unlike the stiff or folding type scales (rulers), the compact retractable scales fit nicely in any toolbox.

RULE OF THUMB: A retractable ruler should be 12-feet or longer and have a lock on the front. The lock helps stop the ruler from retracting while you are using it.

THE KNIFE FAMILY

#24: Common Shears

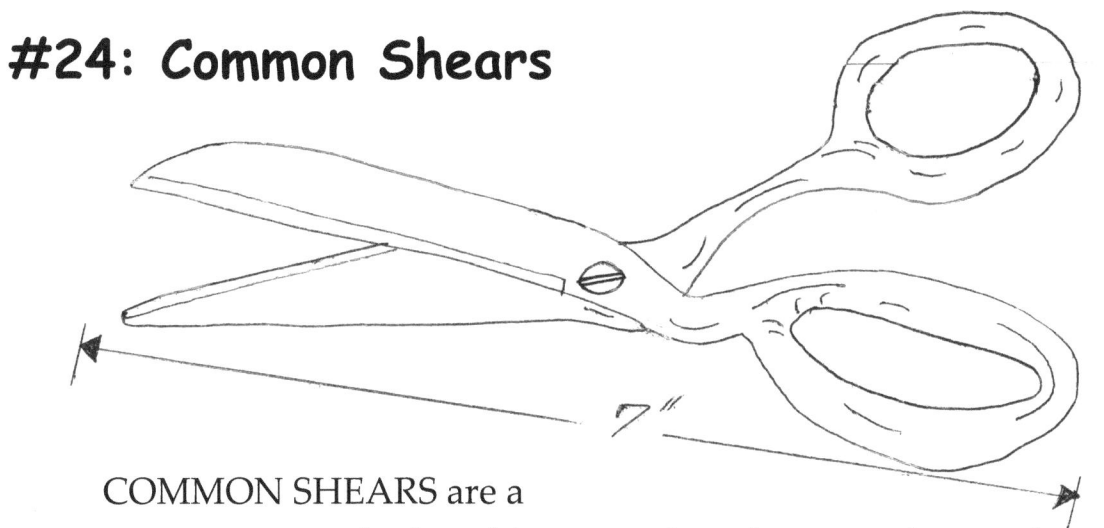

COMMON SHEARS are a must, to cut paper and other things – such as the materal on packages.

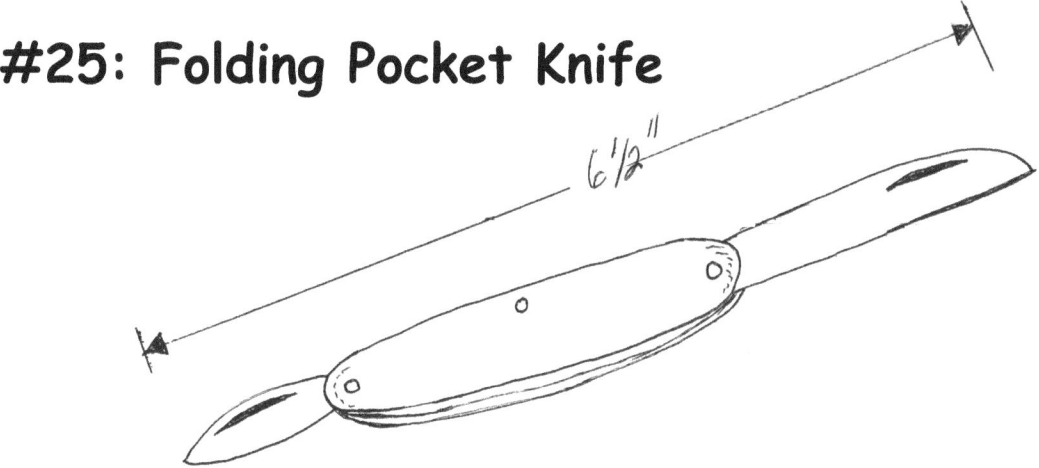 *RULE OF THUMB: The scissors can be fairly inexpensive and sometimes can be found at yard sales. Plastic handles are O.K.*

#25: Folding Pocket Knife

FOLDING POCKET KNIVES cut easiest when sharp. You need only one or two blades on your pocket knife. Ask someone to show you the safety tips below for handling a knife.

RULE OF THUMB SAFETY TIPS: Watch that your fingers don't get between the blade and the case when closing the knife. Don't cut toward anyone or yourself. Always clean and close the knife when you are finished with it.

#26: Carpet Knife - Retractable

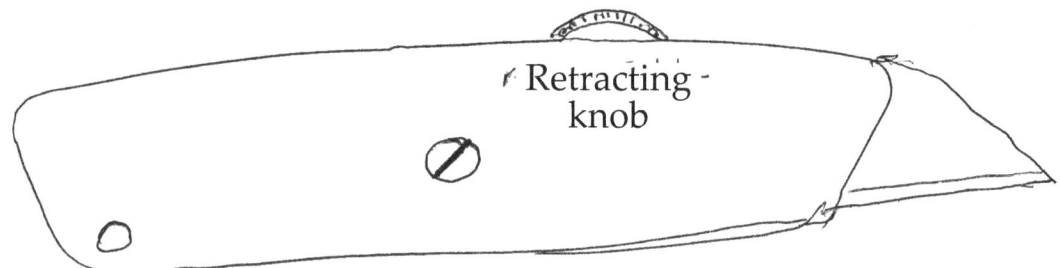

CARPET KNIVES are designed to cut rugs and carpets. They have very sharp razor-style blades and are great for cutting thin plastic and cardboard.

 RULE OF THUMB: Always retract the sharp blade when done.

#27: Multi-Tool

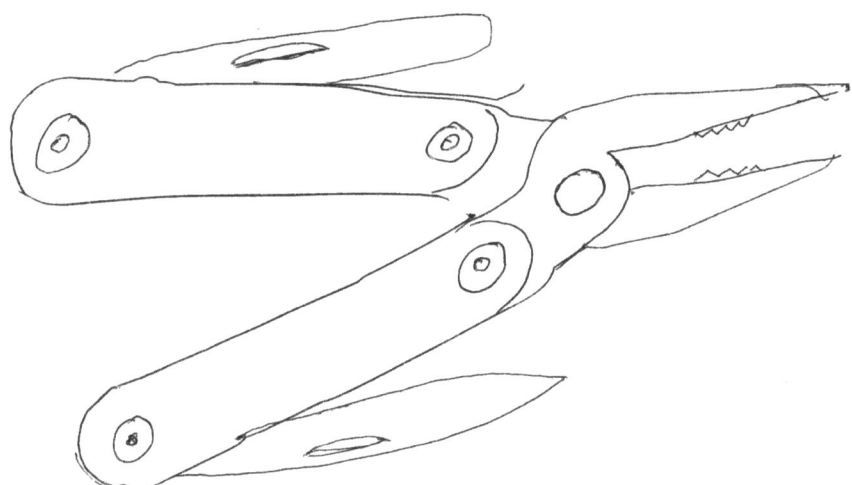

MULTI TOOLS are a must for your basic tool box, because they are so handy. They have files, screw drives, and some have scissors and knives.

 RULE OF THUMB: Stainless steel multi-tools won't rust when wet. With so many moving parts, plain steel rusts and is soon useless.

#28 Whetstone, or Sharpening Stone

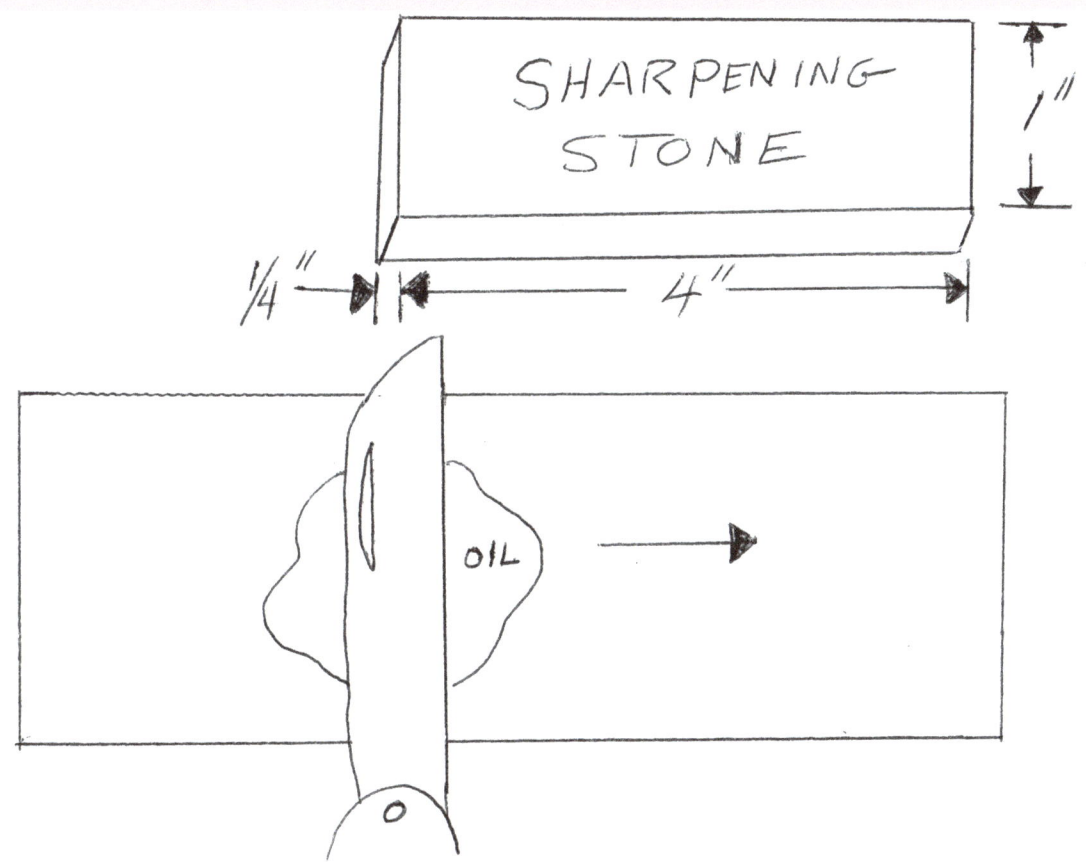

WHETSTONES will break if dropped as they are made of sandstone. Three-in-one oil can be used when sharpening. The oil stops wear and tear of the stone. Sharpening of your knife takes place when you try to shave a tiny layer of stone off the whetstone with your knife blade. Do this in one direction only. Lift the blade and turn the blade over and come back up the stone. This sharpens the other side of the blade.

RULE OF THUMB: Small whetstones are fine. White whetstones are the best. Use plenty of oil to wash the stone as you sharpen your knife. BE SURE A GROWNUP HELPS YOU WHEN YOU PRACTICE THIS SKILL. Always wipe the whetstone clean when done, and before you put it in your tool box.

THE FLASHLIGHT FAMILY

#29: Flashlight

NEW - LED Lites are inexpensive, small, and very bright.

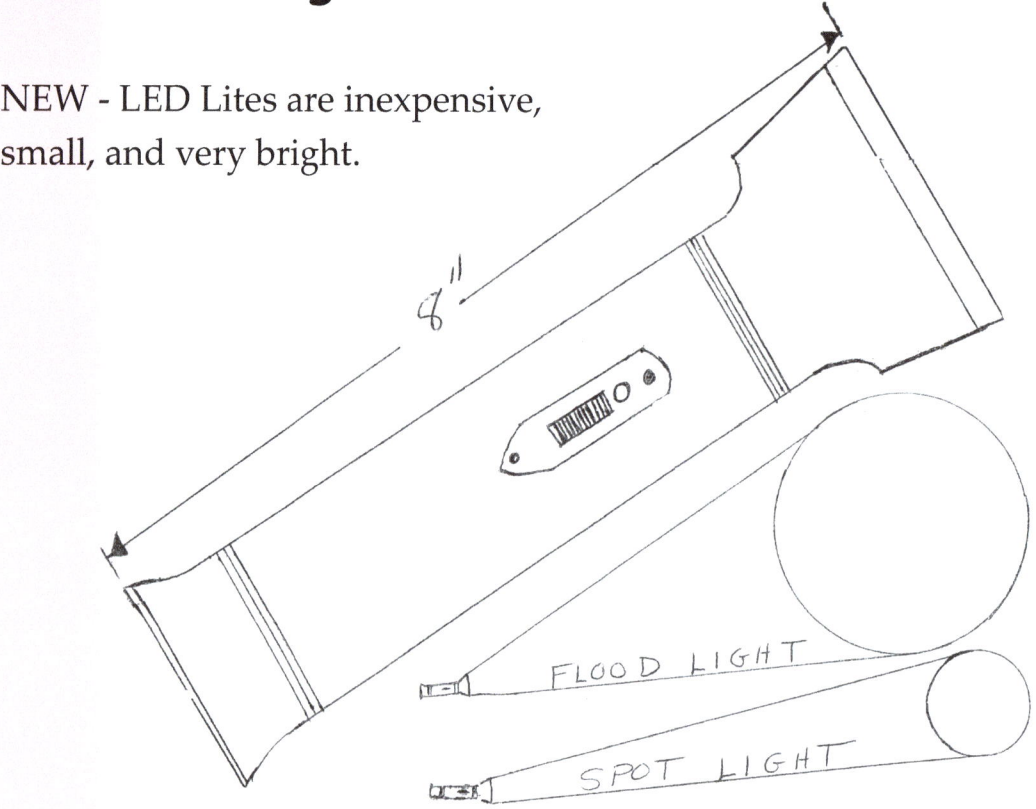

FLASHLIGHTS are very common and you may even own one. Something you may not know is that there are several types of flashlights, spotlights and floodlights. It is best to have a spot flashlight in your basic toolbox. The new LED flashlights are awesome ... the batteries last longer and LEDs are much brighter.

RULE OF THUMB: If batteries are wet or leaking liquid, recycle them and then wash your hands immediately afterwards. Don't put your hands on yourself or anything else until after you wash them, because batteries leak acid when they are dead, and battery acid is very dangerous – it can burn the skin and eat through clothing. Get a light-colored flashlight (yellow or white), as it makes it easier to find when you need one.

LITTLE HARDWARE STORE

#30: Multi-Drawer Parts Caddy

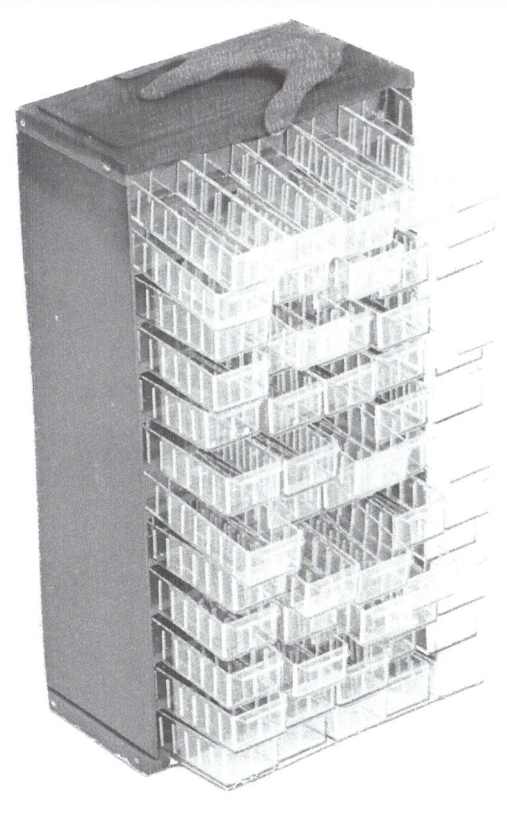

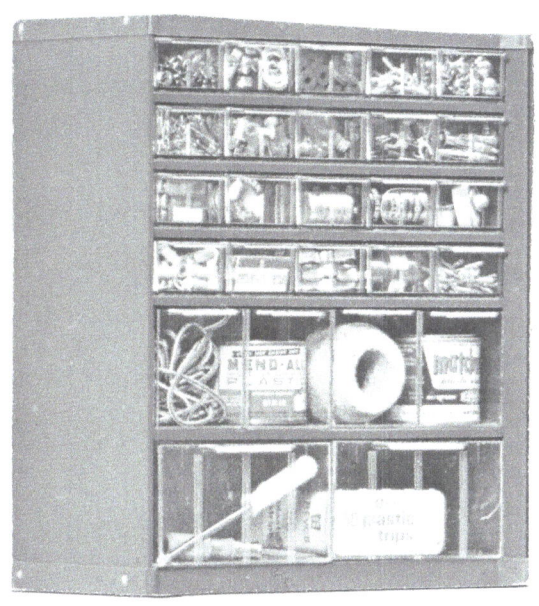

THE PARTS CADDY organizes your whole world – all of your parts such as nuts, bolts, washers, springs, and even cotton swabs. Besides your basic tool box, you need to have a parts caddy like the one above.

RULE OF THUMB: Stick-on labels are also handy. Write on each label then stick it on the end of the drawer, so you will know what is in them. Each Parts Caddy should have at least 40 separate drawers.

TOOL CARE
10 Best ways to take good care of your tools

Owning your own tools brings some added responsibilities. Follow the steps below and they will guide you and make it fun to take good care of your tools.

1. After using each tool, return it to your toolbox.

2. Make a special place in your toolbox for each tool. Smaller ones should go in the top tray, and large ones underneath.

3. Keep your tools clean by wiping them off after each use.

4. Broken tools need to be replaced or repaired as soon as possible.

5. Use the tool that fits. A large nut can be easily taken off with an 8-inch adjustable wrench – not with a small pair of common pliers!

6. Keep track of each tool. It is probably best not to lend your tools, as you may need them before they are returned.

7. Never leave tools outside overnight. Steel tools will rust easily and moisture will ruin them. Plus, you may forget where you put them.

8. Put your toolbox in a dry place. Off the floor is best, and on a work bench or in your car trunk would be just fine.

9. Learn all you can about your tools . . . who made them, where and when they were made. It's just fun to know. Finding out about these things, would be a great project for school.

10. Lock your toolbox as tools are very valuable and should last you all your life. A combination lock eliminates the need for lots of keys.

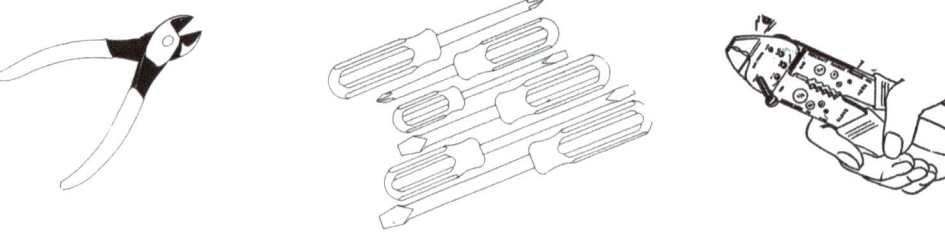

PRACTICE FOR TOOL USE
BY TAKING SOMETHING APART

I want each of you to ask your mom, dad, teacher, or friend, to give you one of the following items that is broken – don't forget to say "please" when asking – a radio, clock, blender, coffee maker, toaster oven, old typewriter, adding machine, old record player, lamp, fan, or most any small appliance.

IMPORTANT!

"Before we start, I want to tell you that we are going to follow some basic safety guidelines that all people need to use when tearing things apart."

First: you will NOT be using any electricity.
Second: we are NOT going to break or handle glass.
Third: we are only going to do this with the help of a grownup.

A. First we find a clean, well-lighted area in which to work, such as a table, work bench or countertop. Make sure you put cardboard or newspapers down. If you are tearing apart a heavy item like an adding machine, spread an old towel, cardboard or cloth over the rug or floor to protect them, as sharp, hard edges will ruin these in minutes!

B. Find about 12 empty plastic containers. We will not use glass jars because they could break.

C. Using tape, label each container with one of the following names (a grownup can help you with this): washers, nuts, bolts, sheet metal screws, springs, wire, switches, feet, knobs, tubes, misc. parts.

D. OK, now we're ready! Oh, good idea ... go to the bathroom, maybe have a snack to eat and drink, because a *BASIC RULE OF THUMB IS:* Things go better when we are ready to begin. Ha Ha, have a short nap, too. Mr. Fix-it did!

So, are you ready? Let's begin!

1. First, take the feet off of the item you are working on. Try a Phillips screwdriver or, how about a Nut Driver? Take off the back, top, bottom and sides. Don't forget to sort the parts into a container, dish, or parts bin. BOY! This is fun!!!

2. Now we remove the cord! Use your Common Pliers. Slide the pliers open to the widest position and grab hold and pull. Wow! You did it! Now get your Wire Cutters and cut the wires.

3. Inside at last! look around. Do you seen any springs? OK, now use your Long-nose Pliers. That's it, take off the spring and put it into your spring bin.

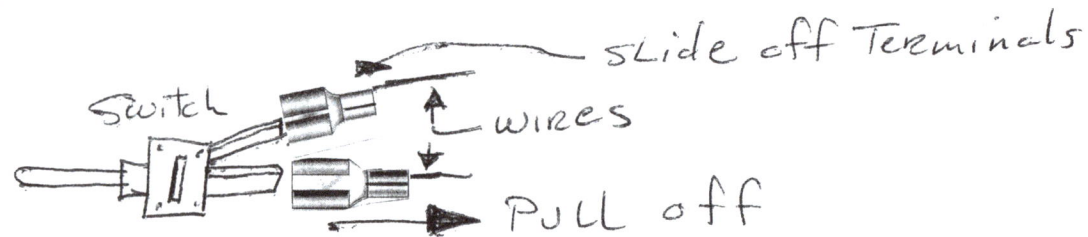

4. Switches, like the one above, have slide-on terminals. Just pull them off with your fingers, or use your Common Pliers. Use Wire Cutters to cut the wires.

5. (About one hour later) ... Hey, you little whipper-snappers, you did OK! Look at all the pieces and parts in the bins ... WOW!

6. Now sort and put similar small parts into your Parts Caddy and lable each drawer with the name of the part you put in it. Recycle the appliance cases and large body parts.

   And now here is a question for you to answer: *Why do we keep all these parts?* The answer is that they may come in handy for fixing another small appliance or toy. For example, let's say your favorite pull wagon lost both a nut and a bolt and the handle fell off. Having a Parts Caddy makes it easy to find what you need to repair your wagon, because most nuts and bolts and screws are made to fit many different things, and you didn't have to go buy them!

HARDWARE

We call the parts that you have stored in your Parts Caddy, "HARDWARE." This is where the name came from for your local "hardware" store. Maybe you can visit a hardware store sometime and see all the kinds of hardware that this kind of store has in its bins and caddies.

Just think, by storing the parts in your own caddy that you have just torn off your broken item, you now have your very own little hardware store!

7. Now it it time to clean up. Follow the steps to putting your tools away, and remember to clean up the whole work area.

YOU ALL DID JUST SUPER!

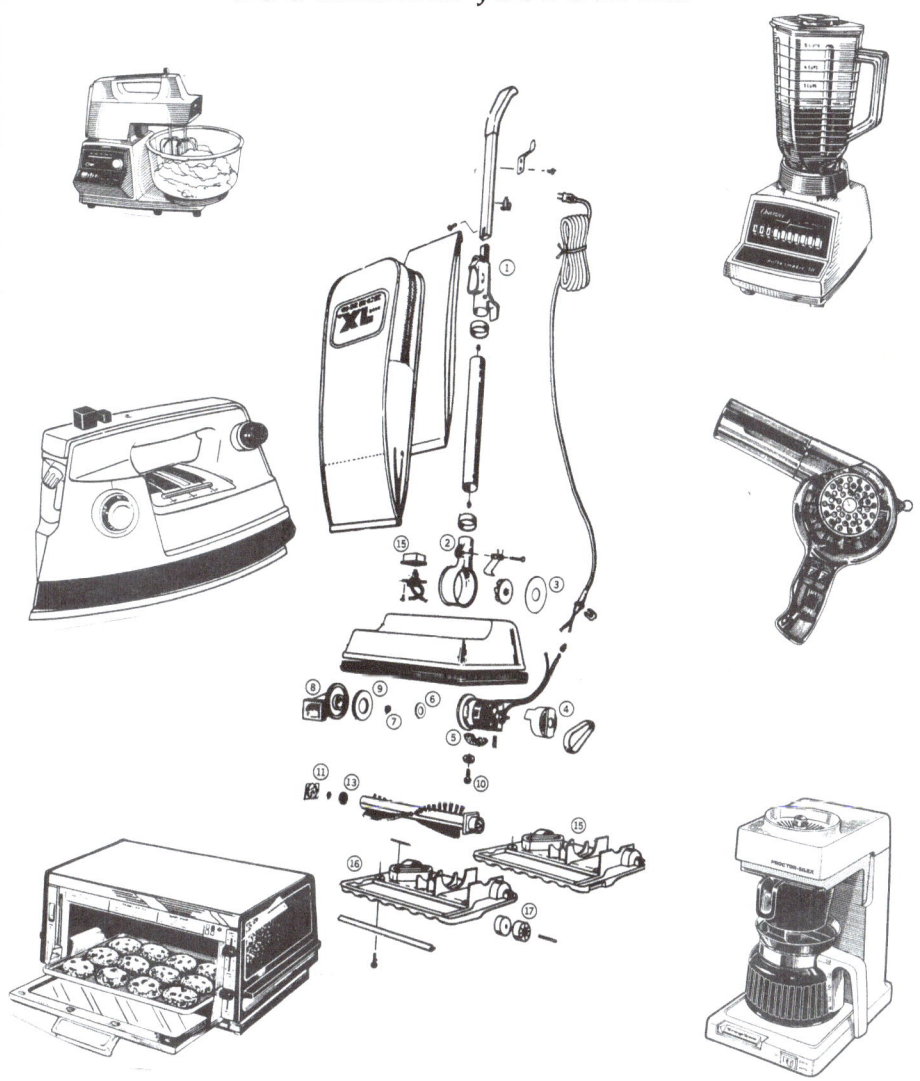

TOOL HANDLING SKILLS AND KNOWLEDGE
Playing Detective

We all like playing games, so in this section we are all going to play detective. You will be shown basic hand tools, common household items like cleaners and oils, and also common hardware. As a good detective, your job will be to find and correctly identify the items described. Are you ready to start? Let's see who is the best detective.

JUST AN EXAMPLE:

There is a grease that is used on steel gears in electric kitchen mixers, and also in electric power tools. We call it "lubricating grease" and it is made from oil out of oil wells in the ground. Grease is not used on plastic parts or plastic gears because it softens them and will ruin them.

Vaseline or silicon spray are common household products used to soften our skin when we rub on a little. It is also used as grease substitute to lubricate plastic parts.

QUESTION: Can you find a jar of vaseline? Wow, wasn't that easy? Now put it back in the same place as you found it and we will try to find the next item.

1. HARDWARE:

Common screws are easy to find. A common screw has only one slot on its head.

Q. Can you find a common screw in your room? Very good, you did.

A. If you have not found one yet, here are clues: look at a light switch cover, a door or drawer. Screws hold on most knobs and handles.

2. SCREWDRIVER:

Q. What screwdriver would you use to remove a common screw?

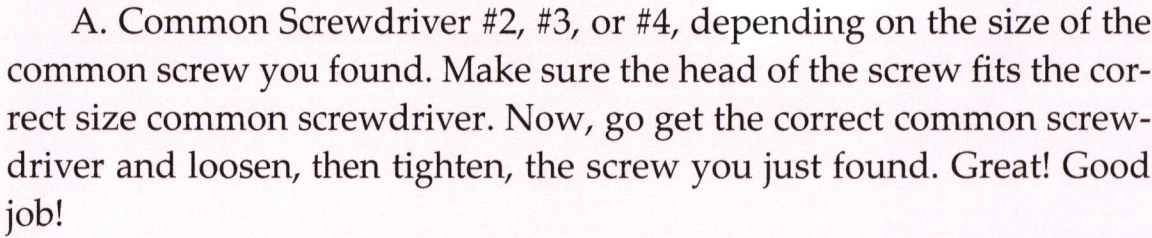

A. Common Screwdriver #2, #3, or #4, depending on the size of the common screw you found. Make sure the head of the screw fits the correct size common screwdriver. Now, go get the correct common screwdriver and loosen, then tighten, the screw you just found. Great! Good job!

3. PHILLIPS SCREWS:

Phillips screws have a crossed slot (+) on their heads and look like this

Can you find one on your door? Can you find one on the top of your hot and cold water faucets, or under your toaster?

Q. What tool do we use to take them out or put them in?

A. A Phillips screwdriver, #5 or #6.

4. MULTI-TIP SCREWDRIVERS:

Multi-tip screwdrivers have a special thing that not many tools can do.

Q. What is the multi-tip screwdriver's secret?

A. It is magnetic. Wow! It can pick things up by just touching them.

Q. What WON'T a magnet pick up?

A. Paper, plastic, a sponge, pencils, and many other things that you can test out on your own later.

5. JEWELER'S SCREWDRIVERS:

Jeweler's screwdrivers are very tiny and have small ends to fit in small common and Phillips screws.

Q. Jeweler's screwdrivers are used to repair what items?

CLUE: Do you wear glasses? Does anyone you know have an electric razor or small radio?

A. All of the items above have small screws that your jeweler's screwdriver will fit.

6. HAMMER:

Hammers come in all shapes and sizes. Now it is your turn to choose one for your toolbox.

Q. Which one would you choose?

> A. Real small one
> B. Real big one
> C. One that fits your hand and that you can lift easily.

A. The answer is C. Yes, it is very important for you to easily handle your hammer. If you choose one that fits just right, your hammer will be your friend for a long time.

7. PLIERS:

There are many different kinds of pliers, but for your first toolbox, you only need the ones mentioned in this book. Common pliers will hold many things in their mouths. They have lots of teeth and can grip really well.

Q. Can you use common pliers to hold a piece of wire?

A. Yes you can and it holds really well, too!

Vise-Grips are pliers that will hold many things in their jaws, too, but some have a secret screw that adjusts to open and close the jaws.

Q. Where is the vise-grip size adjustment screw?

    A. Back of the pliers

    B. Bottom

    C. Front

A. The answer is A – the back of the pliers. See page 14 for a picture.

Q. What releases the lock of the vise-grips when you want to remove the vise-grips from a locked position?

A. The release tab.

For those of you who have not found the release tab, you can also look in your book at the picture Tool #12. Be careful when you press on the release tab, because the vise-grips will open very quickly. You might want to practice with your new tool before locking it too tightly. Or, obtain one of the more modern vise grips without the locking release tab. They work very well, too.

Wire Cutter Pliers are used to cut round wire.

Q. If a wire is too big for wire cutters, how do you cut the wire?

A. Use your hacksaw, #10. Hold the wire with your vise-grips, #12.

To practice this, you should have a grownup help you.

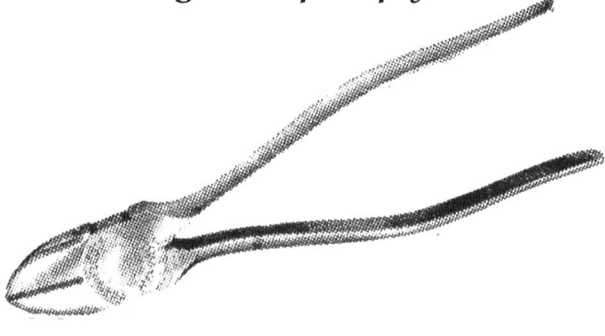

Stak-On Pliers are special because they do SO many things.

Q. Name one of the things they can do.

A. If you said they can cut wire, that is a correct answer. They can also cut bolts, squash (crimp) stak-on and strip insulation off of wires.

Beth asks, "What is a sta-kon?"

A stak-on looks like the parts pictured at right. They are hollow pieces of metal that slide over a piece of wire, and are used to connect wire to an appliance's switch.

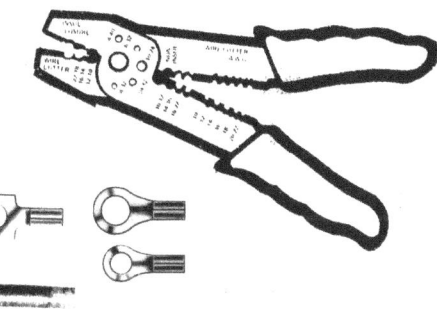

8.   SCRIBES, PUNCHES, CENTER PUNCHES:

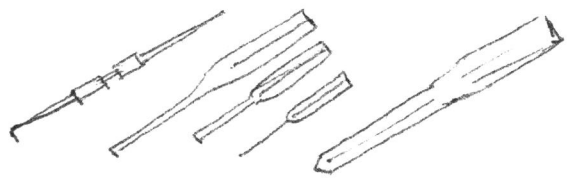

All of the above tools are round metal and are used to line up holes or start holes or find holes.

Scribes are sharp at both ends.

Q. Are BOTH ends or a scribe straight?

A. No, one end is bent.

Punches come in assorted sizes and have flat ends. These are not listed as basic tools, but you should know what they look like.

Center Punches have a point on the small end. To start a hole, or to start a screw, you should first use a Center Punch to make a small hole so that it is easier to put the screw in. To make the small hole, place the point of the Center Punch on the place where you want to put your screw. Tap the end of the Center Punch lightly with your hammer.

Q. What happens when you tap the Center Punch with your hammer?

A. That's right ... the small end of the punch makes a tiny hole in the wood, plastic or metal. The tiny hole makes it easier for the screw to go in.

9. FILES:

Most files are made from hardened steel and have teeth all over them.

Ignition Files are inexpensive and come in very handy when you have to work on something very small.

Q. Ignition files are very _____ compared with most files.

A. The answer is "small". The Ignition File is very small, but important to have in your first toolbox.

10. WRENCHES:

There are so many different kinds of wrenches that we cannot mention all of them in this book of basic tools. Besides, the only one you need in your toolbox, is the 8-inch adjustable wrench, #20.

Use one hand to hold the wrench, and the other hand to adjust the size you want, by turning the small wheel by the mouth.

Q. The 8-inch adjustable wrench would be used on what kinds of hardware?

A. All nuts, large and small, would need an adjustable wrench.

11. FLASHLIGHTS:

Good detectives remember things. Can you remember the two types of flashlights that are most common? Remember that we talked about flashlights in the section on the Toolbox Family? The two types are "spot" and "flood" flashlights. New LED lights are small and very bright.

Q. Can you remember what type of flashlight you should have in your toolbox?

A. It should be a spotlight type of flashlight.

12. THE PARTS CADDY

The Parts Caddy is used to store what kinds of things? All kinds of parts.

 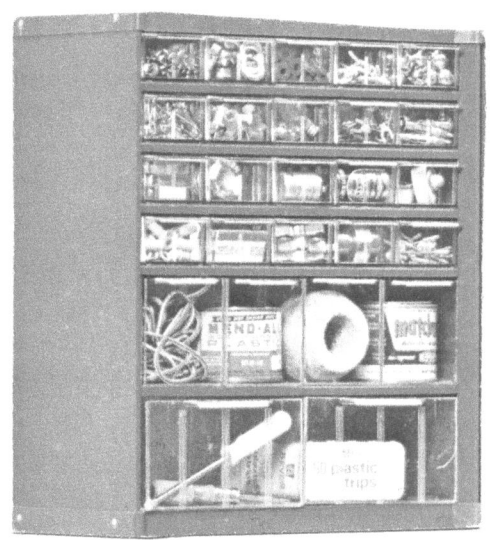

You are all very good at playing the detective game! Now that you know how to play detective, you can make up your own questions about your tools, and have fun asking your friends if they know the answers.

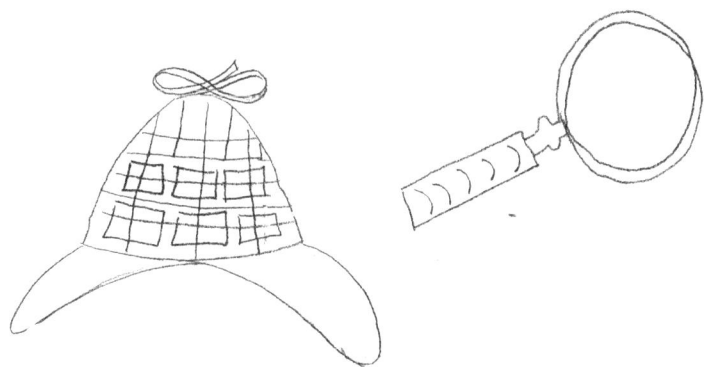

GOODBYE FOR NOW

To Everyone from 5 to 95!

Working with you and showing you the basic tools, has brought a lot of happiness to me. With these basic tools and skills, you will quickly build confidence.

You now know how to use your new friends – your basic hand tools – and you know how they work. That is great! I am very proud of you for coming this far.

In a short period of time, you will also start to put many things back together that you, or someone else, has taken apart. Watch closely how others work, what tools they use, and also remember the little tricks I have told you about in this book.

Slowly, but surely, you will find that you are fixing things. At that time, I would like you to make a drawing of the first thing you have fixed and send it to me so I can see how well you have learned to use your basic tools. You can send it to: Roger's email: rogerdrafter@comcast.net.

Always remember to clean up the whole area where you have been working, and put your tools away. The job is never finished until the workroom is picked up and clean. Also, the job is never finished until you are clean, too, so it is now time to clean your work area, and YOU!

So long for now. Happy fixing!

Mr. Fix it

www.ingramcontent.com/pod-product-compliance
Lightning Source LLC
Chambersburg PA
CBHW041523280526

45792CB00004B/1357